This series edited by
DANIELE RIVIERE

IN THE SAME SERIES

Jean-Claude Gallotta
Groupe Emile Dubois
by
Laurence Louppe
Jean Louis Schefer
Claude-Henri Buffard

Daniel Larrieu
Compagnie Astrakan
by
Gilbert Lascault
Daniel Dobbels
Nadia Tazi

© EDITIONS DIS VOIR
3, RUE BEAUTREILLIS
75004 PARIS

ISBN 2-906571-28-8

TRACES OF DANCE

Drawings and Notations of Choreographers

Edited by

LAURENCE LOUPPE

Translated from the French by

BRIAN HOLMES

(PREFACE - IMPERFECTIONS OF PAPERS -
GRAVITATIONAL SPACE - FEUILLET'S THINKING)

PETER CARRIER

(LIFE SCORES - NOTATIONS AND DRAWINGS -
NOTES - BIBLIOGRAPHY - NOTATION ORGANIZATIONS - PHOTOS INDEX)

We would like to thank everyone who helped us to produce this book, specially Laurence Louppe who supervised its production
Bernard Blistene who assisted us with the original French version,
Catherine Louveau, Marion Chopin.

and

Belgium

Anne Teresa De Keersmaeker, Bruxelles — Roxane Huilmand, Wolfgang Kolb, Bruxelles

Canada

Thecla Schiphorst, Simon Frazer University, Vancouver — Chantal Pontbriand, Montréal

United States

Madeleine Nichols, Monica Moslay, the New York Public Library, Dance Collection —
Nikolais Louis Foundation for Dance, New York — Margarete Roeder Gallery and Merce Cunningham Foundation, New York —
Yvonne Rainer, New York — Simone Forti, Vermont — Trisha Brown, New York — Meredith Monk, New York —
Lucinda Childs, New York — Dana Reitz, New York —
Julie Graham et Lynne Addison, Paula Cooper Gallery, New York — Dance Notation Bureau, New York — Art Service, New York — Anne Chivot, services cultu-
rels de l'Ambassade de France, New York — Ohio State University, Colombus — Alain Sinturel et Gérald du Manoir, New York

France

Emmanuel Le Roy Ladurie, Marie-Noelle Roy, Bibliothèque Nationale, Paris —
Martine Kahane, Patricia Damour, Bibliothèque de l'Opéra, Paris —
Bibliothèque Mazarine, Paris — Bibliothèque Inguimbertine, Carpentras — Bibliothèque Municipale, Lyon —
Jacqueline Challet-Haas, Marion Bastien, CNEM, Crépy-en-Valois — Jean Pomarès, Paris — Dany Lévêque, Paris —
Marseille Objectif Danse — Xavier Douroux, Eric Colliard, Centre d'Art Contemporain, "Le Consortium", Dijon —
Elizabeth Guelton et Corinne Boquet, Paris — Jean-François Lemarchand, Angers —
François Barré, Dominique Bozo, Ramon Tio Bellido, Paris —
Odile Duboc, Paris — Daniel Larrieu, Paris — Philippe Decouflé, Paris — Georges Appaix, Paris —
Dominique Bagouet, Montpellier — Hervé Robbe, Paris —
Régine Chopinot, Michel Salat, La Rochelle — Jean-Marc Matos, Toulouse —
Monique Duquesne, Paris, Isabelle Ginot, Paris — Marie-Laure Violette, Paris —

Germany

Archives Mary Wigman, Akademie der Kunst, Berlin Ms Erlekamm —
Dr. Ulrike Gauss, Staatsgalerie, Stuttgart

Great Britain

Valérie Preston-Dunlop, Andrea Philips, Christophe de Marigny, The Laban Centre, London —
The British Library London — Rambert Dance Company —
Els Grelinger, London

Swizerland

Harald Szeemann, Kunsthaus, Zurich

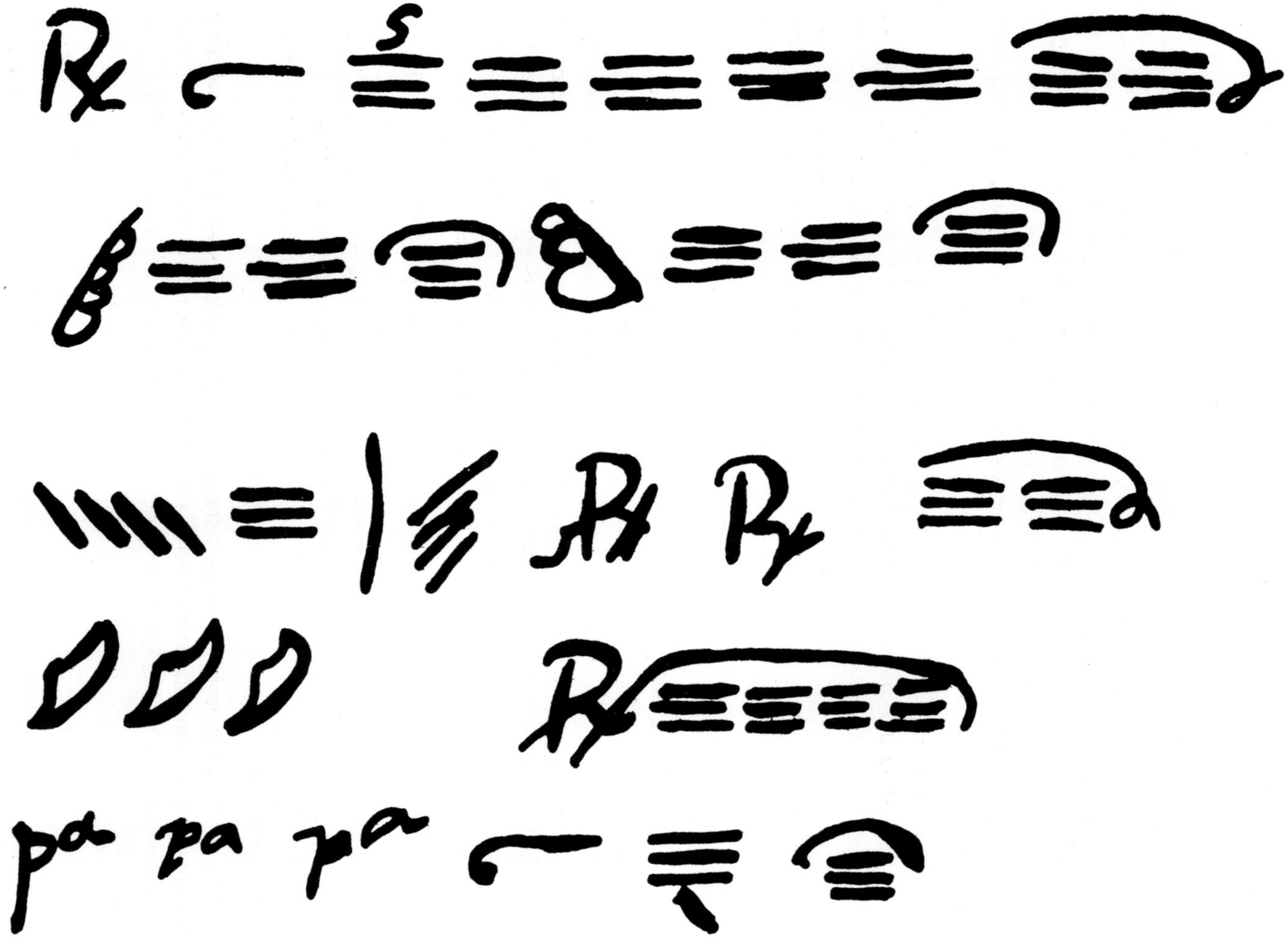
pa pa pa

PREFAGE

The drawings and notations of choreographers are little known. They result from a more or less private practice, limited to a small professional community, or sometimes even from the secret, intimate pursuits of their authors. And yet whether they are coded systems aspiring to universal value, or pure graphic activities linked to personal inspiration and impulsion, these documents harbor a force of expression, a visual energy related to the body and the movement that gave them birth.

It is this largely unknown corpus that *Traces of Dance* proposes to bring to light. But this proposal implies no claim to establish the history of dance notations. An invaluable study by Anne Hutchinson-Guest has already retraced the unfolding of this strange adventure of the human mind and body[1]. The need to pay homage to her research goes hand in hand, for us, with the intention to distinguish our project from hers. By bringing before the public eye these objects of an extreme rarity, as fragile and indefinable in their cultural status as in their appearance, we invite the viewer to an aesthetic contemplation above all, to a sensitive encounter with the example of these traces charged with emotion.

In this way, the drawings and notations of choreographers can interest the entire range of critical inquiries linked to the question of sight, which, at this century's turn, seems increasingly to bear on the limits of the imaginary — both to question its nature, and to mark its borders, or sometimes its cracks. Midway between choreographic tool and work of art, between the most refined drawing and the incomplete sketch of 'another stage' to be designated uniquely as possibility, these documents reach beyond the internal questions of dance, to the tenuous frontier of meaning where the strategies of the symbolic come into (or out of) play.

◀ 1

To lead the reader's thought and gaze through this undiscovered realm of the imaginary, we have appealed to several points of view, to several types of speech and writing. The different perceptual domains traversed by these notations from the system to the work of art, from the conceptualization of movement to its pure emotional reflection in a graphic medium form the objects of historical, scientific, and artistic approaches, linked in varying degrees to the specific practices of dance.

Since this field has never before been treated on such an ample scale in France, we felt it indispensable to add an important complement of bibliographical references and other information capable of enriching and illuminating an experience which, we hope, will be reflective and poetic above all.

Laurence Louppe

7

N.B. double cette a...

**chiquenaudes
Notes 82**

Profil Profil Profil

sous les seins
main derrière le dos

Tête gauche droite -
B tient la tête
A tient le coude de B

.tape main

face-dessus

Mains
tenues dans le dos.

poing toujours tape . +
pojoje.

deja doigt
fois avec d...
phases.

Buste penché

Main traînante

cris d'index
dem... avec / hanches.

battement de coude

coup d'index

IMPERFECTIONS IN THE PAPER

Among the great arts of time — music, literature, and dance — the latter is the only one, in the West, to have maintained a continuing relation with oral tradition. This mode of transmission, which has largely disappeared from the canons of our culture and is judged primitive by some, even though it is fully operative in other very complex musical traditions, remains linked to the history of dance, and even more, to its very identity. Dance can have no recourse to the sign, for its essence is to forego the *detour* that leads there. The access to dance, whether it be perceptual or interpretative, is a direct access that surges up from the heart of matter, from the heart of emotion, above all in contemporary dance. Dance is lived and traversed as a living present; it has, in appearance, no need for a symbolizing system that would be incompatible with experiential givens and would reduce the sensible fabric of movement to an all-resuming graph, universal, transferrable from one place to another, from one textuality to another. Movement is necessarily punctual. Though it may be analyzed or qualified, it can never coalesce from a determined stock of lexical elements which would furnish its texture or definition. Even in the great school traditions, which operate on a fixed vocabulary, the miracle of dance is to transcend the gestural glossary through the poetic emanation of an *event*, unique in color and intensity. Even when fixed in advance, its vocation is to rediscover what Trisha Brown calls "the innocence of the first act"[1]: the gift of dance is to be immersed in its own sensation without any immediate need for an orientation, for a formal categorization.

◄ 2

At its source, the movement of contemporary dance is multiple: formless, it reposes in the infinite sweep of its possible germinations. Its force and clarity require it to shed, at the moment of its emergence, all the parasites that could alter or deflect its course, even if this course is still shaken by counter-tensions. But in the intimate fibre of its dynamic, it retains the shadow of the possibilities that gave it birth. From its unfurling springs the flood of "phantom movements" whose accumulated impulsion it preserves, as in certain paintings where one sees the painter's "regrets," shades that haunt the final composition, clinging after-images of the could-have-been. For dance, and above all contemporary dance, does not produce definitive figures. It provokes *acts*. We know that the analysis and transmission of *acts* does not come about through the *sign*, but rather through the contamination of "states" whose movement develops the degrees and qualities of energy, its tonalities. The reading, the capture of such givens can only be immediate. It suffers no delay, nor any passage through a grid of translation. Movement is most certainly readable, but its phrases are be grasped flush with the organic and perceptual tissue that gives them birth.

At the moment when the first inklings of what is now called contemporary dance appeared, in the person of Loie Fuller, on European stages — in the course of the 1890s — Mallarmé dreamed of dance as a "poem unburdened of scribal accessories"[2]. A counter-writing, the reverse of any grapheme, dance would lead to the abolition of the Letter, opening up the supreme space of the poem, wherein nothing but a pure whiteness without content is inscribed. Only the organic can approach the threshold of this space swept clear of signs, only movement can designate it and, simultaneously, what is most unattainable in it: the possibility "to arrive by physical means to the most impalpable realm of thought." Mary Wigman's wish could seem paradoxical. It is only the resonance of a boundless aspiration. The dance: endless journey beyond inscription.

Mallarmé's phrase was no more than the visionary disclosure of what was about to occur before his eyes. Fuller revealed dance as a poetic state, moving and colorful, a permanent return to the source of all dynamics, escaping from the traditional definitions of art and thus consigning to failure any attempt to name the flaming energies of the body, to enclose them in a concept. Contemporary dance was born, an art without scribe, a voyage of wavering dynamics and trajectories. Isadora Duncan would no more search to capture its contours in a tightly clasped container, than Rodin would seek to retain the overflowing masses of stone within a peripheral limit. A new stage emerges for dance, where it is less the sign than the very process of signification that dissolves. This is not the formulation of another language. It is a transformation of re-presentation itself. It is a *trajectory* between the real and the sign. This trajectory is perturbed by the presence of a living body, intervening as such. Representation supposes the absence of the object, the absence of being. Here, life inhabits what will never be its icon or its index. Dance de-represents[3]; it courses through zones of perception where meaning can only be invented amidst the debris of signification. To return danced movement to a site of inscription is therefore grave. It amounts to the reimposition of a figure from which dance had slipped free. It also amounts to the reconstruction of a representational architecture whose restraints had been broken, whose frame had been burst...

And yet the site of inscription — wherein hover, mysterious shadows, the accessories of the scribe — has always, almost fatally, been bound to the destiny of Western dance. Better: its inscription is what dance inscribes. For dance only became a poem without a scribe through the absorption of the Graph into itself, all the way into its own organic and subjective tissue. Mallarmé himself foresaw this[4]: the dancer, in his work, becomes "Signe" or "Cygne" [swan], a whiteness, an obstinate presence in the sedimentations of time and space, which petrifies in the icy mirror of the rigid, completed act. In the transmission of the name, in the permanence of the ancestor, in what founds the present moment. Daniel Dobbels reads the invisible, indecipherable "gramma" that we hear in the name Graham (Graham = gram = gramma, the letter)[5]. A secret dilemma tense in the heart of dance. The notion and activity of "choreography," as understood in the different meanings this word has assumed over the centuries, is unique to the West (we will return to this point). In this writing of the overall organization of space, does life not seek to decrypt its own letter?

In Canto XVIII of *Paradise*, in a passage with which choreologists are quite familiar, Dante invites the reader to contemplate a strange spectacle: supernatural creatures, each bearing a flame, move singing through the heavens. At the end of each musical phrase, they regroup and form a letter of the alphabet or a heraldic symbol[6]. There we witness, in detail, what three centuries later will become an important procedure of the early baroque "ballet": the danced movement stops at the end of each musical

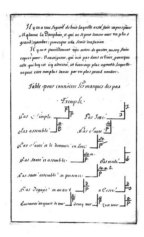

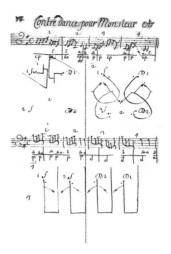

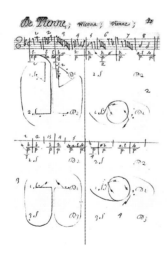

sequence, and the unfolding of the dance leads to the constitution of a planimetric figure that the audience can read from above. The poet shamelessly anticipates our chronologies, and his premature description pays no heed to the decrees of dance history, which will fix the official birth of such practices much later, in the Renaissance. Thus he invites us to step back yet further from the purely historical field wherein these enigmas are formulated, wherein these analogies weave their threads. It is of little moment, for us, whether Dante could have really witnessed such a performance in his own time. The site of dance circulates through Time, it haunts both the real and the imaginary. Seen from far off, or up close, the stage of the dance belongs less to an objective reality than to a moving surface of writing, a kind of nowhere without fixed base, in which bodies assemble and unfasten a mysterious geometry. (Thus in Dante's text, under the steps of the celestial dancers, the three stems of the lily, symbol of Florence, spread out to form the M of Mary, which vanishes in turn into the night.) In this visionary evocation we rediscover all that founds the Western conception of dance: the quest for a sign inscribed in matter, for the cartography of a "text" which movement will read in a space it does not know. ◄ 3 As if even before worldly matter had achieved its organization of the visible and invisible, it already contained an inherent "letter," like the *Vowels* of Rimbaud's poem, a sign that is latent in organic tissue as well. This writing, as we have seen, has no previously instituted support: it disperses in all dimensions, it is interior to every anatomy, to every kineosphere. Perhaps the world's writing insinuates itself into the course of the heavenly lights, as suggested in the Zohar (on the basis of a Judeo-Arabic source, with which Dante was no doubt familiar). Maybe it wanders still today, through the "imperfections in the paper" that Merce Cunningham scrutinizes in the pages of his notebooks, deciphering innate dances. Far from being one chance procedure among the others that Cunningham uses, these traces would then be an immanent writing, an autonomous composition that the paper bears within itself, even before human intervention lays down the slightest sign. As if what allowed itself to show through here, on the surface of a sheet of paper observed in its transparency, were all the possible surfaces that movement haunts in their very texture, yet still leaves blank, unmarked.

To choreograph is, originally, to trace or to note down dance. This is the meaning that Feuillet, the inventor of the word, assigns it in 1700, in the title of his work *Choreography, or the art of describing dance with demonstrative characters, figures, and signs* (The French title contains a savorous hesitation in spelling, a delight for the modern semiotician: we read "*l'art de d'écrire*," almost as if, in English, one were to read "the art of de-scribing..."). Since Feuillet's time, the acceptation of the term has undergone a singular evolution, and today "choreography" refers, not to the activity of notation, but rather to the creation of dance, or to "composition," as is also said in the Anglo-Saxon world. Numerous elements encouraged this semantic mutation: among others, one must point to the influence of Rudolf von Laban, a great admirer of Feuillet, who contributed to a reintroduction of the latter's vocabulary to the stage of modern dance. It is certainly not through any concern for etymological legitimation that we recall the presence of the idea of notation, of tracing, in the creative act of dance. But one cannot help observing that to designate the creator of dance, the West has favored the word that refers to the presence of the scribe within, the one

4 ▶

who measures, consigns, registers, and above all archives. This presence stems from an irreversible inheritance that contemporary dance finds forever in its possession, in its very practice and in the concepts that designate it, despite its will for a clean break, despite its aspiration to liberty and independence with respect to the written. It is as if the letter, the diffuse textuality inscribed in life, had immediately — and since time immemorial — impressed its seal on the heart of the destiny of dance, an invisible sign which movement and its projection in space will little by little decipher, transcending the mark.

To compose, to create in dance, is designated in French by the verb *écrire*, to write. Choreographic writing has nothing to do with notation, in appearance at least. A choreographer is said to have produced a very "written" work, without having ever laid down the slightest line on paper, or at least, without foregrounding any such practice. Choreography, for the contemporary creator, corresponds to a transformation of latent motor organizations, of the time and space that they contain, and of the play of exchange between these interior polyphonies and the objective spatio-temporal

Pure movement is a movement that has no other
connotations. It is not functional or pantomimic.
Mechanical body actions like bending, straightening
or rotating would qualify as pure movement providing
the context was neutral. I use pure movement as
a kind of breakdown of the visual experiences. I
also use quirky personal gestures, things that
have specific meaning to me but which may appear
abstract to others. I use both pure and everyday
gestures and don't care whether anyone can figure out
whether one is which, as long as it prompts
them to look. I want to hand
left to the everyday movement
use into me,
and make
an

Oct 76   Trisha Brown

givens with which, among other things, the act confronts them. It is therefore above all a matter of an interior score, moving and intimate. This score is within all of us: it is the ensemble of breathings, pulsations, emotive discharges or mass displacements which are focused on our bodies. It is the geography of the influxes diffused around us by the imaginary vision of space, it is the quality of the relations that we can have with the objective givens of the real — the very givens that movement "sculpts"[7], embraces or disperses according to its own axes of intensity. Such perhaps is the real configuration of the "gram" that constitutes us: an organic, non-figurative writing, a "splashing"[8]. This "splashing" would then be what is carried along in the process called "motility": a certain quality of movement (and of thought in this movement) that allows us to traverse autonomous and limitless regions of the imaginary, making us full-fledged "subjects" without having to constitute us in fixed bodies, armed and insensitive[9]. This is the finality of choreography today, whatever the procedures, the discourses, the stylistic options that accompany it. So it comes forth from the work of an artist like Trisha Brown, so it was invented, exalted, by Mary Wigman in the quest for an absolute poetic movement, with no other figural legitimation than its own energy, in the motor configuration of its emotional source[10]. Thus it is understandable that, faced with such an irreducible tool, the contemporary dancer and choreographer plunged more deeply in their practice than any other creator should need to use a relay surface, a conjunctive tissue between the body, its movement, and the space of projection where the inner score can unfurl. Regardless of the way it is used (project or memorization), the essential thing is to see this surface as the limit of the scriptural, the tracing of what the letter does not say, but where another text shows through, another reading of living substance. The status of these markings is necessarily anonymous and secret. They will follow the general fate of dance notations, which is to escape almost always from the public eye, whether because the public is not interested (and here we rediscover the phenomenon of the "exclusion of the visible" described by Didi-Hubermann with reference to the "boti" of Santa Annunziata in Florence), or because the very destiny of the choreographer's "papers" requires them to remain invisible, to concretize an intermediary *state* between the object of vision and the object of non-vision, to designate in the obscure history of notation (but also through the very nature of the notational process) a blind spot, a suspension of perception.

Here we are are surely quite far from the idea of notation as nomenclature, as archival technique, a neutral and public way of deciphering danced movement. But choreographers' drawings also form part of this story. They participate, with or without the consent of their authors, in a long scriptural history by which movement has sought to inscribe itself and to remain in memory, that is, *in the world*. The drawing in no way represents a final twisting, the sensible metamorphosis of an initial aim or a semiotic displacement motivated by a desire for exhibition in a museum, as occurs with other types of notation that have long since acquired the character and force of an institution. Manuscript musical notations, the bearers of scrawls and fevers, pulsations of the hand that traced them, can easily be deflected from their initial, essentially functional status as acts of recording, in order to highlight their graphic and emotive value. This is all the more true in that numerous contemporary composers, regretting the barrenness of classical sheet music, now compose their scores in the form of diagrams, landscapes, linear apocalypses, whose intent is at times deliberately pictorial, as in the work of Morton Feldman or John Cage. An important exhibition at the Staadt Gallerie of Stuttgart in 1986 presented these new visual objects[11]. The same is true for Picasso's writings, tight, obstinate, scratching graphemes which were exhibited at Musée Picasso in Paris in 1989, as an activity carried out alongside painting, but sharing its visual impact and impulse, contaminated by the graphic storm of the oeuvre, a subset and relay of the pure plastic gesture.

Such presentations gain their force from the ambiguous relations that these documents maintain with the official histories of institutionalized forms of writing; and it could well be that the displacement of the word and the letter to the center of the plastic arts, as practiced in our century from Magritte and Klee to Broodthaers and Haacke, proceeds from a similar ambiguity[12].

All the more so as these signs can also figure a mysterious writing, a secret, indecipherable code, no doubt enveloping essential rhythms and symbols which cannot be reached by any denotation. As such, they can be integrated to the image, as in the work of videast Gary Hill where they become a speech from before all images, a

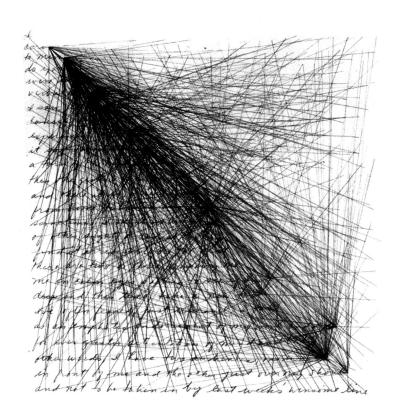

Sololos
Oct 80

Trisha Brown

speech from before all speech, a kind of matrix of gnosis, attaching itself to the roots of the imaginary.

Even if they too are bearers of this type of combined event, where the entanglements of preexisting elements furrow new lines of reading, dance notations are of a very different nature, and above all, have a very different destiny. Because they are perfectly unknown, the state of surprise that their discovery provokes does not need to be redoubled by an effect of deflection. One cannot deflect from an accustomed usage that which has already been deflected, or rather, that which history has rejected. Dance notations have no precise cultural status, they occupy no place of authority or of symbolically invested reference. The scribe of dance is a quite small and modest scribe, provisional and without posterity. He scribbles his "hieroglyphs" (as Feuillet puts it) in the shadows of writing. Aside from the baroque period, at the hinge-point of the seventeenth and eighteenth centuries, it must be recognized that dance notations have never been the object of official interest, and even less of institutional interest. They form no lineages, all the way until Laban's notation. For no stabilizing power, no corporative interest ever opposed their incessant transformation. No councillor, no clerk or federation of typographers ever bound them in place, on the strength of conviction and for particular advantage, unlike verbal and musical notation. Bachelor machines, linked in each case to a specific choreographic language itself destined to disappear, they have disappeared as well, traces even more evanescent than the phenomenon they sought to account for. Their genealogical tree cannot be drawn. Despite certain rare influences they have formed no trunk, aside from the systems generated by Laban's, who in this respect remains the great inseminator of contemporary dance. Almost all the systems for the writing of movement are born not of an inheritance, but of a solitary and profoundly orphaned uneasiness or fury. Thus one can well understand that the larger human community, so often indifferent to the existence and the importance of its own movement — and therefore, no doubt, indifferent to dance[13] — should show no interest in systems of notation. But this disinterest touches even the dance community[14].

It would be superficial and reductive to dwell on the punctual, factual aspects of

◀ 5

the rejection of notation by dancers. Independently of the historical context in which the dancer's practice has evolved, far short of the subjective and sensible instances which *keep him in the present*, there is, plunging deep within him, not an instantaneous expressivity but rather a kind of archaic fear, linking back to a far more buried, even immemorial stratum of experience, a fear whose signs are already manifest in history.

If the famous "druidic alphabet" used to mark the dance figures executed in the ballet hall and inscribed in the libretto is indeed related to the "Celtic" or esoteric figures current in the early baroque period, one cannot ignore the fact that the druidic religion, of which Julius Caesar gave such a savage description, *forbade writing*. Do the figures of the dance then represent this interdiction or its transgression? Does every writing, every codex of movement, refer to the law or its deviation? Does writing refer to the death sentence of the process in its designation (as Derrida described it in his *Grammatology*), or on the contrary, to the limit, to the traversal of this stopping-point? Karsavina, the recalcitrant student of an austere tutor's courses in the Stepanov notation system at the Imperial School of Dance, would in later years write in her memoirs that these traces were "cabalistic signs of black magic"[15]. Thus a captivating and deadly power intervenes in these "hieroglyphs" of dance notation, in this ancient scrawl whose unreadability goes hand in hand with its excessive and mysterious power. Does something then die or fade away like bodies made victim to a spell, is something lost in the very conquest of its memory, in the quest for an invisible writing, for a sign that must be ripped from the body of the dancer, torn forth from his creative power?

It will be said that the notation of a dance does treason to its emotion and to the urgency of a present moment, to a real transferal of energy; it will be said that what comes about in danced movement — what is "torn" out there, far more than simply manifested — cannot be translated, cannot be brought back, is linked to its pure emotional and physical actualization, which no sign can restore, which no sign has even the right to inscribe as a definitive event in the annals of human time. These arguments are current, I have already evoked them in another form. In my view there is

6 ▶

CHOREGRAPHIE
OU
L'ART DE DE'CRIRE
LA DANCE,

PAR CARACTERES, FIGURES
ET SIGNES DEMONSTRATIFS,

c lesquels on apprend facilement de soy-même toutes
sortes de Dances.

rage tres-utile aux Maîtres à Dancer & à toutes les personnes qui
s'appliquent à la Dance.

Par M. FEUILLET, Maître de Dance.

A PARIS,

cz l'Auteur, ruë de Buffi, Faubourg S. Germain, à la Cour Imperiale.
Et chez MICHEL BRUNET, dans la grande Salle du Palais,
au Mercure galant.

M. DCC.

AVEC PRIVILEGE DU ROY.

E. 361 (1)

Quand une page aura plus de Pas, & de Nottes qu'il n'y a de lettres dans l'alphabet, au defaut des lettres, on se servira de chifre 1 2 3 4, &c.
On remarquera que comme les lettres de l'alphabet & les chiffres ne
seroient pas suffisans pour marquer tous les Pas d'une Dance particuliere-
ment quand elle est bien longue, on recommencera à chaque page à
marquer par A B C D, &c. & continuer ainsi de page en page.

De la Figure.

ON doit remarquer deux sortes de figures dans la Dance, sçavoir
figure reguliere & figure irreguliere.
La figure reguliere est quand deux ou plusieurs Danceurs vont par
mouvement contraire, c'est à dire que tandis que l'un va à droit, l'autre va à gauche.

EXEMPLE.
Figure reguliere.

La figure irreguliere est quand les deux Danceurs qui figurent ensemble vont tous deux d'un même côté.

EXEMPLE.
Figure irreguliere.

Je dis donc que lors que dans une dance on dance quelque espace
de temps en une même place, on ne doit plus regarder le chemin que
comme le conducteur des Pas & non de la Figure ; mais quand la Dance
va toujours & ne reste point en place, pour lors on doit regarder le
Chemin non seulement comme le conducteur des Pas, mais encore de
la Figure : or donc pour observer cette figure, il faut après s'être placé
au commencement du Chemin, sur lequel on doit dancer, de la ma-
niere qu'il a été enseigné à la page 35, il faut, dis-je, voir si la figure est
droite, diametralle, circulaire ou oblique, si elle va en avant, en arriere,
ou de côté, soit à droit ou à gauche, comme il a été démontré dans les
Marches pages 37, 39, & 40. puis après avoir appris l'Air qui doit être
notté au haut de chaque page, ou fait jetter ou chanter par quelqu'un,
on ajustera les Pas avec la Mesure, comme il a été enseigné cy-devant en
parlant de la mesure, & on fera la figure en dançant, telle qu'elle est
démontrée sur le papier.

Quand il arrivera que les Chemins se croiseront les uns au travers
des autres, il faudra que les Pas de l'un ou de l'autre laissent une distance ou brêche suffisante, pour laisser passer les Pas de l'autre Chemin, afin d'éviter la confusion qu'ils feroient, s'ils se mêloient les uns
parmy les autres.

EXEMPLE.

something much more grave here, something much stronger, drawing its resources from the double notion of the *Law* that seems to impose notation and the *Interdiction* whose object notation so clearly becomes. And this paradox stems from the fact that the dancer is a veritable avatar of Orpheus: *he has no right to turn back on his course, lest he be denied the object of his quest*. Into the subterranean night of his body are projected all the myths of fateful unveiling: Psyche revealing the mystery of desire; the fruit of the knowledge of good and evil. The dancer is imprisoned in "the innocence of the first act." All his force serves only to nourish and to renew this innocence. All his force gathers in this limitation. Like the great mystics, he remains on the margins of revelation, in the shadow of a night which has nothing "fusional" about it: for it is but the threshold of this abandonment, beyond which the work of the body may begin.

Why then is writing an obsession (both literally and metaphorically)? Why, across centuries of Western culture, this obstinate quest to weigh the depth of the night's darkness, to measure the intermittences of its light, to seize the trace of its invisibility, always questing for a sign that would traverse the night?

Why all these drawings, tracings, planes, grids, trajectories cast on paper by a hand rich with its own movement, as if the movement of the hand had read the movement of the body, and projected its flux? Why all these crumpled, yellowed, forgotten papers, found in the choreographer's dwelling or elsewhere, in the diverse and inaccessible sites of the archives of dance? Poor papers, so often, like the bits of wrapping or tracing paper on which Mary Wigman set her uprooted landscapes, without scale or reference point. Like the old programs where Merce Cunningham scratches out his grids or his animal heads. Like the lined or squared schoolchild's paper used by Dorris Humphrey, Yvonne Rainer, or Dominique Bagouet. Scrawled working notes? Of a project, of a memorization, of a floating form of writing which has not yet invented its surface?

The paper in no way retains a record of the dance, it retains a trace which itself cannot be consigned anywhere else. It retains the upsurge where the interior score assumes a figure. The body does not write it, for it writes the body. Even when they come from professionals and friends of an expressive fever, these papers are always inhabited by something beyond the visible. They are scattered leaves of paper, transiting between the "mirror-sheet" and the "body-sheet" (to borrow Sami Ali's terms[16]). Mirrors without a doubt, but also membranes, skins, the interface of porous spaces. The site of the illusory transaction between inside and outside, the metaphor of that final bodily envelope which is the surface of inscription or of painting, and which is only the prolongation of the cutaneous and intercutaneous elements determining the conjunctive territories of the imaginary. Scattered pages, you are but the ultimate skin where the body reads the limit of its own sensation: in you, a dialogue is engaged with a possible vertigo, with a flow of weight into space, with an impulse that frees the visibility of a springing tension, a bursting energy, a phaseless figure of speed or rotation...

Writings, systems, drawings, it matters little: they all must be discovered and followed through notation's long, laggard assimilation of the sign asleep in the body. What does this sign say, what does it account for? At first, it knew not: the sign to be read in the body knew not of what it was the sign. It was searching for itself, as sign and as body. It only took form in the body's mobility. It had first to trace the figure of this mobility, before discerning the unfigurable. Little by little, it would accept to figure that which escapes all figurability. This is a long, strange story...

I do not mean to trace a "gradus ad Parnassum" whose origins would lie in the shadows of strictly codified dances, inflexible in their vocabulary (though not in their movement), and from which the luminous conquests of the modern era would finally emerge. Each moment of notation has had its flashes of astounding intuition, but has also known its regressions, its troubling diminutions. The history of dance notations offers nothing resembling a linear and "progressive" unfolding, no more than the histories of other symbolic practices. Thus the strange fifteenth-century manuscript of the *Basses Danses* of Cerbera and its echoes in a later text of Tarragona reveal a system of astonishing signs, articulated, in the reading of Carles Mas Garcia, along two axes of symbolization: one relative to the disposition of movement in space, the other to the graphic stylization of the lexeme that designates this movement in language[17].

One can always point to the low artistic impact of a repertory of ball dances addressed to the cultivated aristocracy of Catalonia, or to the limited number of fully constituted and therefore coded figures to which these graphemes refer, as well as the linear, processional, and purely directional aspect with which they are seemingly concerned. But the combinatory system we find here, the form of writing, the treatment of space as a rising wall where the dancing body advances towards a rift in the sky, everything here is troubling, surprising, provoking questions about space and sign, and about the genius of the scribe who was able to invent, at the dawn of the Renaissance, a system of representation that is wholly unique in the period.

And at the far end of this history's unfolding there is — for those who would refuse the terms of progressive evolution — something that tears profoundly within the unattainable realm that previous notations had only designated. An anecdote reported by Anne Hutchinson-Guest is eloquent here: visiting Pierre Conté, our explorer (and guide) in the history of notations commented that the Conté system does not register certain directional axes of the extremities, a troublesome gap for the reading of Anne Humphrey, for example. It does not matter, said Conté in reply: movement has an essential truth that does not depend on the details of configuration. Should his statement be taken as a failing in the system, or on the contrary, as a remarkable breakthrough in consciousness? If the second option is possible, it signals that something has broken out in the twentieth century, that something of the sign has rejoined the necessity of movement, its profound reality. There is something here which no longer gathers up the visual in the closure of a figure; something which, on the contrary, escapes all formal molds, opens up to the experience of movement as the essence of movement. The memory of movement would then be the memory of that which returns in us, of that which makes its return like a wave of life falling back from the shore. The inscription of movement would be memory itself, the shadow cast by experience. It would be the seismography of an intimate unfurling. As the wave is born from another wave, so the body alone can decipher the echoes of a resonance that returns, like a faded percussion in the material of paper, a rhythm that need only be awakened.

To be sure, it is in a very different context, in the Quattrocento, that the West first elaborates the idea of archiving dance through written procedures[18]. This archiving is

diff structures se succèdent
- longueurs différentes
- passages de l'une à l'autre de
manière non systématique :
cul, fondu enchaîné (développement
de la danse ? qui se transforme.)

┌─────────────────────────────────┐
│ Quatuor avant la danse ensemble │
└─────────────────────────────────┘

1) Essayer de réceptionner fred qui tombe
→ 1 passe du duo Sam / fred

Structure qui en mélange un tas, rapidement.
Joue sur les contrastes entre les formes +
que sur leur développement.
→ annonce de structure développée + tard

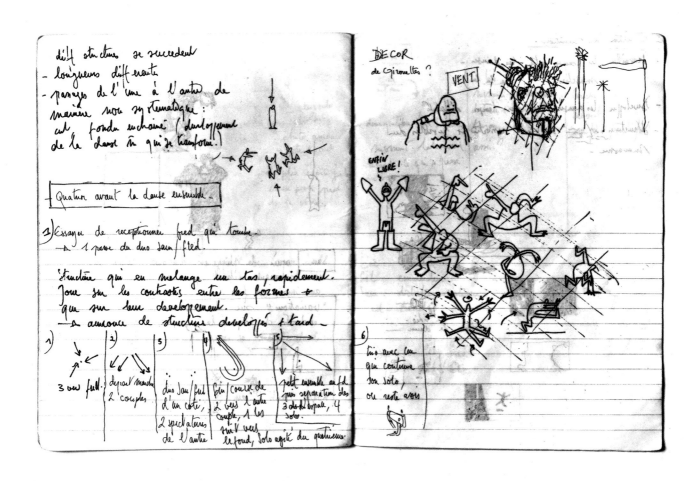

1)
3 vers full

2)
départ marche
2 couples

3)
duo Sam / fred
d'un côté,
2 spectateurs
de l'autre

4)
fin / course de
2 vers l'autre
couple, 1 les
sur V vers
le fond, Solo agité du quatrième

5)
petit ensemble au fd
puis séparation des
3 du fd empale, 4
solo.

6)
trio avec un
qui continue
son solo,
ou reste avec

DÉCOR
de Girouettes ?

VENT

ENFIN
LIBRE !

exactly concomitant with the invention of the choreographic act. To project a movement or a symmetrical interrelation of diverse movements into space means both writing in space and writing on paper. Even as they set out on the conquest of visible territories with which to invest and mark out the imaginary realm, as in cartography and
visual perspective, the dancing masters became the owners, the "authors" as we
would say today, of their "basses danses" or "balli", compositions which will be signed
with names such as Messer Domenico (da Piacenza) or Messer Guglielmo (Ebreo). No
specific signs to invent: a verbal description aligned on a rather simple glossary of rhyth-
mic and motor figures, all ready at hand, is today quite enough to let us read and reconstitute these dances perfectly. Like the rest of Quattrocento art, these notations entered
tranquilly into the reserves of the market, their sublimity intact.

But the sheet of paper on which the imaginary of movement is inscribed cannot in-
definitely remain innocent, like a simple "abaco" notebook wherein the spatio-temporal
dimensions of the figures of human movement would be consigned[19]. The mysteries
borne by this movement are too vast; it could hardly avoid raising the all-embracing questions of social and cosmic space that it potentially contains, even when limited by the
codes of cultivated dance. Rapidly, the renewal of sign systems implied by dance notation is integrated to the ensemble of inquiry into writing and language, as it is posed
throughout the baroque era, from Jakob Böhme to Leibniz, and later, by Jean-Jacques
Rousseau[20]: human anatomy and even physiology, as Michel Foucault read them in his
history of the imaginary at the opening of the seventeenth century, are in correspondence with the very wheels of the universe. The glandular system, among others — so
important today, let us recall, in the work of certain kinesiologists like Bonnie Cohen, for
whom the gland determines the nature and localization of movement[21] — is linked to all
the elements, to all the astral gravities which determine the grand ballet of the universe
evoked by Father Mersenne. Danced movement as it appears in the first court ballets is
therefore the deciphering of arcana, similar to the magical language of the world sought
by the Rosecrucians[22]. It is the premonition of a writing without "language," which
draws its signs directly out of formless matter. Dance in its turn will come to trace on
the surface of paper all that which the body's movement sets resonating in the deeper
regions of consciousness, where no word can reach.

8 ▶

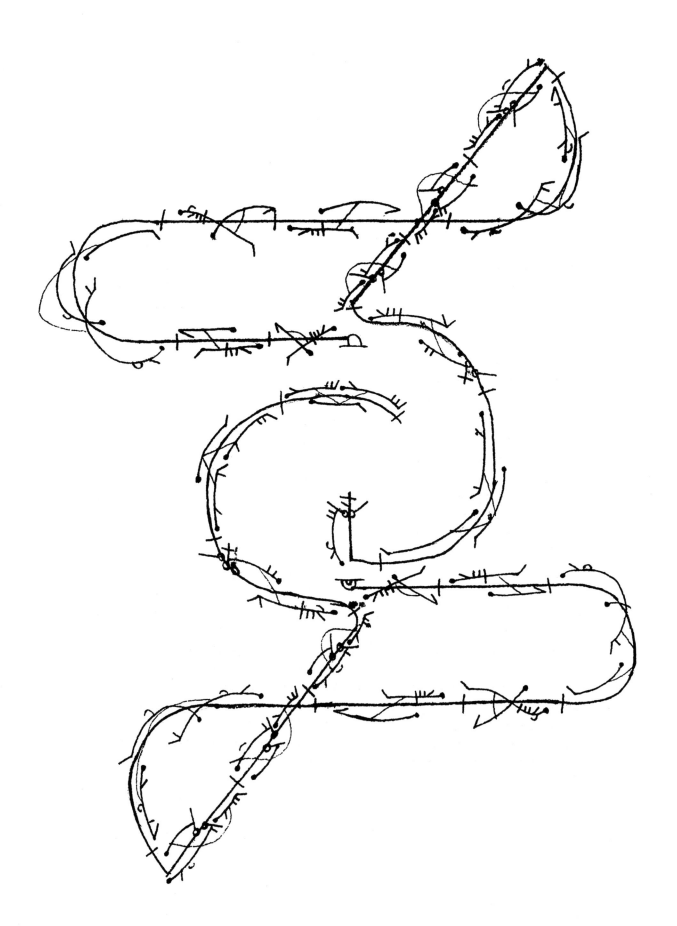

And what of the Feuillet writing system, born with the classicists' return to rationalism[23]? Does it refer to the baroque dancers' quest for "another script," the script which traces, as early as 1581, the essentially symbolical geometric figures (isosceles triangles, circles, spirals, etc.) of the *Ballet Comique de la Reine*? To compose, in the West, means rewriting the world. It is still true today, despite the breach in time that is modernity. For Feuillet, who appeared at the far end of the seventeenth century, it was enough to mark the world; but he marked it in a singularly beautiful way, impressing matter with feathery traces which the world's surface seems barely to restrain from flight. In one of his finest treatises, in 1721, the dancing master John Weaver described this writing with a metaphor both poetic and concrete, calling it the traces of "steps in the snow or the dust." What the earth's surface retains of human passage, the imprint of its successive support-points, is destined to disappear like movement itself. The ephemeral is within the world, and human trajectories are only inscribed within the general instability of the environment.

The trace, in Feuillet's writing, engages two superimposed orders of representation, which are entirely heterogeneous in nature: 1) The tracing on the floor of a path representing the line of an undulating trajectory; 2) The vertical axis of the body as represented by the same line, as though the human spinal column were projected upwards along the axis of human movement. The thrust of the step, indicating the movement of the free leg on either side of this axis, brings forth another fundamental factor: the lateral and sagittal transferal of weight which, through the alternation of support-points, authors all human displacement. Laban would later be most profoundly impressed by this tremendous discovery, and above all by its formulation in abstract signs, each of which marks the quality of destabilization presiding over the exchange of supports; it is not known whether he discovered Feuillet's *Choreographie* in Paris around 1907, or in Munich, the capital of baroque disequilibria and of the flowing masses of seventeenth century sculpture, more or less contemporary with Feuillet. Whatever the case, in the work of the dancing masters and in the entire culture through which they move, the inscription of the motor sign takes on a considerable importance. As a system of memorization, writing allows for the distribution and communication of dances through space and time. From an initial point of view, it is a matter of teaching everyone the fashionable figures and compositions that are danced in court balls, or of reproducing the "best entrées" of ballets for the stage, to be reinterpreted by current practice. This manner of communicating dance through the intermediary of paper, like a letter or a bottle thrown in the sea, gives even those English dancing masters who are "remoted from London" a sensation of victory over time and space:

"And ev'ry dance in ev'ry clime be read;
By distant masters shall each step be seen,"

rejoices the amiable London poet Soane Jenyns in 1725[24]. Better yet, the sheet of paper literally represents objective space. It is a space oriented by the sign. Again in 1725, Pierre Rameau, author of *Le Maître à danser,* recommends turning the score each time one reaches the far end of a course, so as to begin again in the opposite direction. The sheet of paper follows the dancer's orientation, it becomes a traced partner in a parallel space, it accompanies his movement, precedes it, slips before it in an aerial rush of feathery traits. This multiple concomitance of the spaces of dance eternally restates the problem of paper as a "field," as a mobile surface, a metaphorical soil, calling into question the very existence of real grounds and the orientation of trajectories.

Only in the twentieth century will such profound questions again be posed in such a pertinent way. Laban, whose clandestine and indirect links to Feuillet we have already remarked, will be the first to posit the writing of dance as a consignation, not of formal figures, but of deep sensorial realities which inhabit the human body, or as the ensemble of the organic score on whose basis we conceive space, and project ourselves into it. The first of these givens is weight, whose displacement with respect to the center of gravity — itself mobile — is the source of the entire imaginary vision of the body. Thus Laban's notation will use weight-blocks to mark the passage of gravitational impulses with respect to the axis. For as in Feuillet's system, it is the vertical axis that marks the laterality of the body, whereby the fluctuating discharge of weight will symmetrically circulate. This circulation of weight is the effort that constitutes space

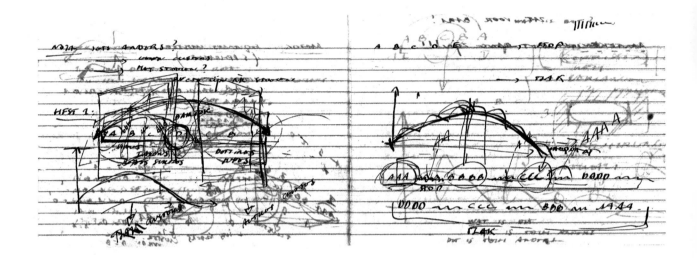

around our own vertigo, on the basis of intensified concentrations of weight at a given place in the continuing mementum. The dimension of the weight-blocks indicates the inner duration of the movement, henceforth free of all cadence, of all exterior signal. Their configuration indicates their directional dynamic, while their degree of coloration (a scale from black to white) designates qualities of intensity and emission (the flux).

In a general way, a multiplicity of proposals for notations of movement will be stimulated by the emergence in the humanities of a consciousness of the "technologies of the body" (to borrow Mauss's expression), conceived as a variety of experience and even as a symbolics quite distinct from other signifying systems; and the process will continue in the ground-breaking discoveries of bio-mechanics and the experiments in time-lapse photography — although very few of the resulting proposals, it must be said, will match the depth and conceptual novelty of Laban's discoveries. Like his, these new notations have the merit of aiming for universality, of attempting to decipher all human movement, beyond any recognizable gestural code. Some will even extend their ambition to the attempt at describing absolute movement, the movement of animals or of nature (Eskhol Wachman). Laban himself noted "the movement" of immobile objects, which, long before Nikolais, he called "motion": a perpetual clinamen of apparently immobile forms, which in their very immobility (the vase, the chair) retain the imprint of the movement and the human energy that gave them birth in labor and pain. In Cunningham's aleatory grids one still sees something of this permanent movement of things, a movement which could be reembodied once more, between two concomitant and dissociated organisations. ◄ 9

But the inscription of movement has not always remained innocent. In 1936, eight hundred performers were grouped together in a Berlin Stadium around a score by Laban. The monumental choral choreography *Neue Freude und Tauwind*, described by Valérie Preston-Dunlop, led the inscription of dance toward the fatal role that it had one day to play, in space and in the history of man. This vast, centralizing gathering was authored by the distribution of a transcription, whose complicity with the Law results from something more than Laban's political unconsciousness (shared by Wigman at that time). Choreography and inscription here rediscover their disquieting role as conquest and occupation, redoubling the abuse of power over bodies as well as territories.

Perhaps there is a significance in the fact that some years later the soldier Nikolais, in the long hours of boredom preceding the Allied landing in Normandy, should have conceived a system of notation not without resemblances to Laban's. Nikolais confided to me that at the time of his crossing to France, his "papers" caused him the greatest concern: he feared he might be accused of transporting secret plans of espionage. A justified fear. For can anyone inventory such counter-spaces with impunity, chart such counter-territories unmarked by any reference-point of the occupying powers, but overrun with labile waves rolling one into the other, linking center and periphery in a constant reversal of movement? Can anyone confront human powers with spaces that are not zones of involuted energy? What the dancer Nikolais here opposes to the world order is an extreme consciousness of human mobility, not as force of attack but as inherent *motion*, as the incessant and multidirectional circulation of living substance, which makes each movement into an ever more infinite trajectory, ever less delimited by space in the form of an institution, in the form of an end-point to the fluctuation of human becoming.

But it was necessary that dance notations, like all writing, once confront the law, so as to rediscover themselves on the far side of inscription as the trial of death. Or better — and this would hold for all the misadventures of modern German dancers in the interwar period — so as to reinvent the outside, the space without which the body cannot know its own gravitational displacement[25]. It was only after this supreme traversal that contemporary dance appeared in France, already burdened, already mined by history. It is perhaps not surprising then to observe what will happen after this supreme outburst of the letter, the culminating moment for all the great notators of the modern era. Through a kind of inward turn that seems to graphically isolate its own figure as though it were the index of a body floating in a boundless space, the young French or Flemish choreographer manifests a desire to return to the body-as-contour, to the anthropomorphic pictograph, whose motor flux had been liberated by modern dance.

There are many ways to interpret the appearance of these small, fragile figures, lost in the sheet of paper without any direct relation to space, or time, like the reoccupation of an existential envelope, at once cutaneous and graphic, as though the line contained the essence of being without any conjunctive rapport to the world. One can, for example, link the segmented aspect of these drawings to the fragmented movement that French dancers inherited from the a certain interpretation of the directional in Cunningham. One can also find here the projection of a state of isolation with respect to living matter, from which the straying figurine is detached, a fetish, a doll, a tiny human hieroglyph, inscribing its silhouette as best it can in the already saturated text of the history of bodies.

But this body, which has forged itself a contour like a graphic carapace allowing it to escape from space, which has become letter or ideogram in order to guard against its own errant poetics, this body today bears something which seems to unbind it. There is a thinking of dance which traverses the protective walls woven in haste among the interwining surfaces that choreography holds back at the limits of the impalpable. Not a thinking which rips apart, but one which links, which irrigates. You see it in the thermic centers of density that Anne Teresa de Keersmaeker lights up like electric discharges in the weave of her own textuality, guided by the intensities of the musical scores that she reads, dwells with, and prolongs in a parallel interpretation provided by the body. You see it again in the drapery that appears in Bagouet's notations, as though an emotive envelope were rolling up space into the movement of bodies, reintegrating the fragment into the continuous fabric of the real.

Scattered papers, tiny surfaces of life, memory-bodies, mirror-bodies, to what mysterious universe does the multitude of your traces refer? Unfinished writings, humble springboards of a virtual space, modest advances beyond the possible, you exist but halfway, in the absence of the body that alone can read you. Incomplete objects, intermediaries between nothingness and life, you are not content like other objects to be the furnishings of reality, or to impress yourself in the imaginary: you leave the order of things but provisionally, the better to transform it. And this without revolution, without fury, content to return, with unflaggingly patient labor, over the minute traces you have laid down at the limits of writing.

figure de la demoiselle en tournant La main gauche, et faisant le tour entier en quittant La main

figure de l'homme en tenant la main gauche en faisant le tour entier et quité la main; / 4 un pas de menuet de coté

4. un pas de menuet de coté

GRAVITATIONAL SPACE

Interview with Laurence Louppe,
Daniel Dobbels

LL: In the course of your teaching activities you became interested in dance notation. That interest, and the importance of your work in general, led us to seek your views on this still largely unexplored question.

PV: It just so happened that in my capacity as a professor of architecture I became interested in choreographic notation. I had a Moroccan student who was working on the subject, and I myself was interested in an architectural measure of space that would be something other than the cut-away plan of a façade, that is to say, a completely abstract vision. Space is movement, it is the quality of a volume, and is therefore very difficult to note down. I became interested in choreographic notation, asking myself if there might not be, in *Labanotation* for example, a manner of qualifying space that

would complement the architect's plans and cross-sections, which are absolutely barbarous things for measuring space, because they don't measure time. But in dance, where the notions of space and time are linked, there is a relativity which translates that reality quite well. Therefore, I must say I got interested in a rather pedagogical way. The student I mentioned, in particular, did a degree on Dance and Space... In architecture people only do geography, and I thought it was high time that the urban or architectural geography represented by the cadaster's plans of the city, by the floor plans of the house, should be completed by a *choreography*, that is to say, a measure of the quality of volumes, in which *Labanotation* would have other functions than that of preparing the body for gestural activity.

LL: You're right at the heart of our preoc-

◄ 10

35

cupations. I'd like to add that Laban saw the body as a kind of score, whose essential ordering principle he called effort, *that is to say the displacement of weight; but this displacement of weight organizes an interior cartography, and even a geography, where the space/time relation already includes an architectural space. When he speaks of "effort shaping," that means constructing space with one's weight, with one's displacement of weight. It is also a geography.*

PV: When I say only a geography, I don't deny its importance. I mean that it must be completed by a measure of movement and not only by a measure of surfaces. In architecture, surfaces are measured but volume is not apprehended at all; it seemed to me that beyond the measure of surfaces there was a measure of time by way of movement, a measure which *Labanotation* could help render. I did not say that his system should be used as is, but that it could inspire architects to qualify the space of movement, the passage, for example, from one level or split-level to the next. When an architect makes a plan he is interested in such things, but he can only measure surfaces, because he has no tools with which to qualify volume.

LL: What you are saying is very impor-

tant, because this idea of apprehending objects not through quantitative measurements but through qualitative criteria is something quite new.

PV: Yes, absolutely. Where architecture is concerned, it is still not at all resolved. I'll take another example. You spoke a moment ago about interior schemas, and it just so happens that I have my students work with mental images. I've been doing exercises for ten years where I make them draw mentally, then graphically. I try to bring the mental vision of the surface, of the space, and its graphic or geographic representation into synch, as we were just saying. This architectural research is not yet finished, but it is headed in the same direction. I might add that I was also very interested in what is called "musigraphy," which means musicians' research into new notations that aren't simply sheet music. That could also serve us as an example. How could architecture use and interpret these techniques in order to complete its traditional approach to space.

DD: What seems important to me is this definition of movement by the displacement of weight, which you designate as "quality." The impression today is that this primordial

Die Ahnen

die Ältesten
und der Weise

Der Weise

Grosses Thema

I Chor: doches aufstehen und
geschlossene Halbkreis (Fächer)
formation nach rechts und links
öffnen

"SALOME" (JUST BEFORE DANCE)

you listen to the parachutists who take these kind of jumps you realize that there are states of perception which change with the acceleration of the fall, on the one hand, and then with the modification of the rapport to the ground. So there is something very complex that happens at the level of the stages before the fall, and they say that very clearly: their vision goes through several modifications right up to the point where it stops changing because they are afraid of going too far, because the ground is too near. There are radically different sequences in free fall. At first the ground doesn't seem to be coming, you have the impression of being in a kind of nirvana, let's say till about three thousand feet; then the ground seems to be coming, that is to say, the tables turn; and then finally it seems to open up. There would be still more stages, but they are beyond human possibility because of the risk of smashing against the ground.

DD: What would be the status of language in this experience? The inertia, the cadaverous state of death is often associated with the fact that the body has no more signifier; is the signifier suspended in this experience, as though between parentheses, or on the contrary, does it fall with the body? One has the impression that in a fall, language falls as well.

PV: There's a word which people don't understand well at all, which is vertigo; you mentioned it just a moment back. In a certain way, excepting chemical vertigo, I mean the dizziness that comes from indigestion or similar phenomena, vertigo is something absolutely unknown. I'd even say vertigo is a blanket term that covers up what vertigo is. I would say that we will only be able to talk about vertigo when we have rehabilitated the being of trajectory. Vertigo is what serves to cover up trajectivity, in a certain way. I'm talking about the trajectivity of the walking or falling man. What interests me beneath this idea that all vision of the world is a fall (literally a fall, which pulls weight along with it), is that we have a perception of the world because we fall into the world. A friend who was about to undergo a liver removal told me, "It's extraordinary, now that my liver is ill it weighs, it's no longer a liver, it's a dead weight." As if something inside him were falling. Not only does the body fall into the world when it is alive, but when an organ begins to lose its life it falls in the body like a dead weight, as though there were an interior weight of the body that

◀ 13

redoubled the exterior weight of the body in the world. In my opinion this is a very interesting element of the materialism of corporeality, corporeality as fall. It lets you rediscover all of religious and mystical thought in a non-metaphorical way: to fall into the body, to fall into matter. It's not a metaphor, it's a concrete thing.

DD: What I hear in your word "trajectif" is "trajet-dit", something said about the trajectory during the moment when the fall comes to pass. Is the consciousness of this speech which is proper to the trajectory bodied forth as such, is the meaning of the gesture said in such a way that it suspends other forms of the speed of the dead weight, other forms of its reduction, of its advent? And in the end, don't you think that in all these systems of notation and even in the very practice of choreography, there is a kind of haunting obsession: to suspend time, in such a way that another time comes to double the dead time?

PV: That brings us back to Husserl and the notion of the living present. There is no time, there is no temporality for someone who is not alive: there is no time for water, for stone. Time only exists for the person who gazes at the stone, who watches the water flow. I think the notion of the living present is very appropriate today, especially when people are talking so much about real time, present time. The real time of technology is only real because there is a living present of the viewer, the listener, or the actor. In effect, then, dance is the putting into operation of the dancer's living present. And this living present is an enigma. It is not the present of the past, or of the future. The living present is without past and without future: it's in the quick, it's in the speed of being in the world, it's in the speed of falling into the world totally so, that is to say, in totality with the body of the dancer, or with the body of the parachutist whom we discussed a moment ago.

DD: But that doesn't just mean ephemerality. I think there is nonetheless some duration in the things you're talking about.

PV: Absolutely, the living present is life itself. It is not a chronological time. It is a "chronoscopic" time, that is to say, the time of presence. And I would say that this kind of time is outside traditional time, the time of tripartition. There is no before/during/after in the living present.

LL: This is what you were saying in an article on real time, published in the journal Psychanalyse.

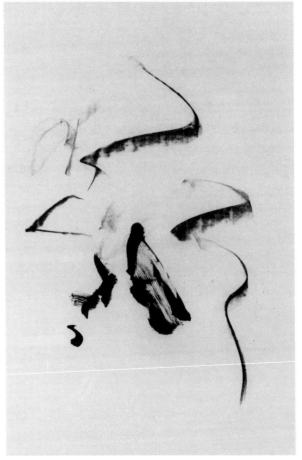

DD: *Right now there is an exhibition on Joss van Cleve, with two representations (one by him and one by Gérard David) of Adam and Eve in their niche, naked, after they have been banished from Paradise.*

PV: We would have to reinterpret the nude, as the fall into appearance.

DD: *What's magnificent with Gérard David is the impression one has that the body, especially Adam's body, is a fall into the world: he is on the edge of the niche, but behind him is a shadow drawn on a gray-blue background, which grows continually thinner as it descends. Could one fall into the world with or without a body? That is also one of the questions of dance. Of course I fall into the world, but maybe I don't fall with the particular body I would need in order to bear up to this rapport with life, with the life that waits for me both as a destiny, in a certain way, and also as an unknown, as an enigma.*

PV: I think that images have a weight. I feel a lot of friction with the people who say the image is nothing, the thing is all that matters. Myself, I'm a weighty image and nothing but an image. There are certain technologies which allow for an acceleration of vision: in a few fractions of a second you're shown a perfectly healthy mouse which decomposes and falls into dust. I find there is a truth in these documents which overcomes any difference between the living mouse and the representation of the mouse. I'm very close to Berkeley in a certain way; I find a lot of very interesting, very relativistic things in his thought. So for me, we are only weighty images. The decline of the image is a decline of reality. To say "the image is nothing, the thing is all that matters" is in a sense to get rid of the thing, to get rid of matter. In my opinion, there is a "tragedy" of the visible (to return to your word "*trajet-dit*") in this misguided realism that we've been caught in for about a century now. The visible is nothing, matter is everything: what does that mean? That means that the image is only valid when you can touch it, or in other words, that you're valorizing a tactile image over a visual or an auditory image. Is a thing more real when I have it in my hand than when I see it? You know we can't accept that, all the more so since there are now "tele-touch" technologies. Therefore you see quite clearly that the image is weighty, that the image is the thing.

DD: *That recalls Léger's* Ballet Mécanique, *the scene where a woman keeps*

◀ 16

◀ 17

going up stairways in such a repetitive way that she finally takes on weight in the image and thus gives the image its real weight. And there is also Bill Viola's work, which shows how a body is always reestablishing its balance and is in fact nothing but pure movement.

PV: Movement is nothing but a maintenance of instability.

DD: What explains the desire to note that instability down?

PV: Why is instability negative? Why have systematizations of movement gotten the better of instability? Because there is, I would say, an old residue of pride, in the Biblical sense of the word, which makes what falls a lesser good, which makes the accident or the attribute less than the substance, and so on. Now I believe exactly the opposite. I believe that the original accident is blessed: we are because we are within an original accident, we are because we are "sinners." Perhaps there is something repressed there, a wrong interpretation of the Bible and of Scripture. For me, it's exactly the contrary. The accident is original, it's at the root of humanness. I am because I am accidental: a man in the midst of falling, a fallible man, that is my grandeur. So you

see, in a certain way the terms of chaos, instability, accident, etc., are terms that are constantly negative even while they constitute us as humans. In reality, we only exist through our failures, we only come to be through our falls, we only are through the accident that is our life itself. This is true of mankind and many other situations we could discuss. And what is interesting in the idea of dance as a fall is that it reintroduces, in a certain way, man as an accident and not as a glorious substance.

DD: And that basis leads him to invent the real.

PV: Yes, to constitute it.

DD: To constitute it, to multiply it, to make it an issue each time.

PV: And there you rediscover an adage of philosophy, largely forgotten these days: "A light doesn't shine without an eye to see it, thunder is silent without an ear to hear it." This table isn't hard without a hand to feel its hardness. So in a certain way the principle of entropy, which is now discussed at the cosmogonic level, reintroduces the notion that man is the observer of the world; but as such, he constitutes it as well. And there you find Berkeley again. That doesn't mean you must speak of immaterialism. That is

48

the problem with the analysis that has been made of Berkeley's thought: it has been completely conflated with immateriality, whereas in my opinion it constitutes a different kind of materialism. Maybe today, through relativity, Einstein's relativity, Berkeley's analyses can be reinterpreted.

LL: If in effect we constitute ourselves in the fall, how should we interpret the idea of the bounce, or of suspense, of holding back? For example, according to Doris Humphrey's work there are two principles in dance, fall and recovery; she said that "movement is an arc of life stretched between two deaths, there is vertical death and horizontal death." Movement is exactly what the curve describes...

PV: It's the trajectory.

LL: The trajectory in its declivity, above the ground.

PV: A parabolic trajectory.

LL: And one which can cut through pedal bases. But how do you situate suspense, and the bounce? How, in regard to this ancient desire of the fall, can we hold ourselves back, suspend ourselves, and bounce? For you, is that a negation of the falling body?

PV: No, not at all, because the horizontal fall, the one that sends you toward the horizon, includes the bounce. The fall mustn't only be understood from up down, it also exists from down up. The bound is an upward fall, just as flight is an assault in reverse. I don't believe there is any center to the fall, except the living present of the dancer. The center is the lived body of the dancer, there is no other center, there is no ground. If you admit that walking is a fall toward the horizon, there is no ground; the ground is relative, its only existence is in the person who falls from high to low. To understand what is meant in the fall by eye, the fall into reality, you would have to try to forget the traditional references of high and low, to situate yourself only in the lived body as the center of time, the center of the living present. And all of today's technologies lead us back to the human body. Tele-technologies mean that man is the center of the world, that the ground has much less importance: thus we have deterritorialization. And the horizon is less important too, as you realize when you see the trans-horizon weapons: radars... In a certain way, the final planet is the lived body, and the lived body is the living present. It isn't a body in the simple materialist sense of the word, it's the

Raum des Gegenrufes
Aufruhr der Toten

living present. Behind desocialization, behind the return of individuality, I think there is in reality the resurgence of man as the center of the world, of man as egocentrism. The conquest of the universe, whether infinitely large or infinitely small, the conquest of space, all technological conquests lead back to "egocentration." And in effect, dance is an art of egocentration. To avoid falling, to turn back and face the audience requires a constant egocentration, as it does in certain sports as well. We come back to the chuteur à vue, who is a kind of planet: he falls into gravity just as the planets mutually attract each other, he is Newtonian.

DD: At this point in your thinking, what would be the status of the presence of others, with regard to this egocentration? Can we fall severally into the world?

PV: That's all we can do, since we are engendered. The fall begins with parental engendering, with the engendering of the social body. I'd say there are many falls. There is the fall into birth; and in certain birthing techniques, the women actually do let the infant fall, it falls at birth. In the same way, society falls on the territorial body; it is projected by the territorial body. If you take

the three bodies: territorial, social, and animal, there is a fall from each into the others. It's because there is a territorial body that the species falls into the world. If this world was not the earth but a planet with x force of gravity, life would have been completely different, our vision of the world would have been completely different. In the same way, the family brings about the fall of the animal body of the infant at birth because the family itself is expelled from the social body, from which it is separated by the love relationship and by marriage, in what I call the populating unity. The populating unity which produces the animal body of the infant at birth is expelled; and from this expulsion springs the importance of the family structure, outside the world, but founding it. How far away the notion of "social class" is from animal, materialist origins! The origin of society is male/female engendering, which is why the current situation of test-tube babies is so serious. You can see that there are three falls. First the fall of the earth into the world, gravity; without gravity there would be no society, the territorial body is fundamental, it is the first weight, the first measure. The second is the social body, that is to say, the species; and the species will engender a couple which becomes the origin of a new

◄ 18

fall into birth. Therefore the movement of falling is global, gravity is everywhere, and it is not a metaphor.

DD: *People talk about offshoots. This is an offshoot.*

PV: Exactly.

LL: *The falling object becomes something very sensible at birth.*

PV: We get back to the problem of my sick friend and his liver, except that here it's a being. When a woman is awaiting childbirth she feels the child weigh, and then it is thrust out.

LL: *And it weighs differently.*

PV: Yes.

LL: *I'd like to broach the question of choreography. You spoke of territoriality. Does a sign have the right to mark this fall onto the territorial, as the tracer-choreographer does? To what extent does it then enter into a mechanism? I'm thinking in particular of Laban's relation to Hitler, when after having sent his scores all over Germany he saw a thousand dancers come to the stadium in Berlin. At that moment Laban became afraid, because he saw that the sign regrouped people beyond his own will, and at great speed, in total instantaneity — because he*

had sent his scores to different gymnastics and dance groups around Germany, and at the same instant, they all came together around a sign. He finally realized that the sign reterritorialized an absolute, centralizing power. I speak of territory because the choreographic territory is not so very metaphorical, it is a real space, after all. Isn't there a danger in the sign?

PV: I think that when you are at the bottom of the pool, pushing off with your feet is one of the elements of the bounce. And if there is no bounce it's because there is no contact among bodies: the feet touching the floor, the bouncing body, the bottom of the pool... This reference seems quite important to me. I didn't know about Laban's relations with Hitler.

LL: *Afterwards he had to leave Germany very quickly.*

PV: It's sure that in nazism there is a very strong rapport to territory: blood and soil are important elements. And it's not surprising that Laban was a focus of emotion, because he cut right to the quick of something essential to nazism. What I mean is that in the ancient myth, even the pagan myth, of the earth mother, there is something that continues to draw me, not in the sense of the

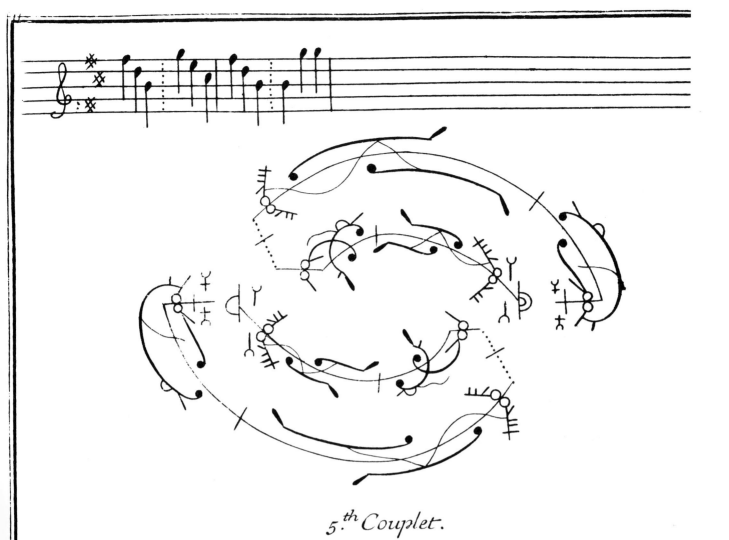

5.th *Couplet.*

ancient goddess, of the "alma mater," but in the sense we just spoke of, the relations of falling that exists between one body and another, between the body of the earth and the body of others, and from the body of others to the birth of the new man or the new woman. What I'm trying to say is that there is a mysterious conjuring of inert elements, something happens between matter and the animate elements, and so my favorite Saint is clearly Francis of Assisi, who said there is a fraternity of the animate and the inanimate. I think that when you say "my brother, the sun" it's not just a pretty phrase, and when you say "my sister, the rain" you voice something of this conjuring of the animate and the inanimate. The dance is an element of this conjuring, in the gesturality of the body: you need the ground in order to bounce, you need the viewer to see what the dancer will not see... Therefore there is a mysterious complicity between the animate and the inanimate which means that you can no longer oppose spiritualism and materialism, and which means that you can reread Berkeley with eyes unprejudiced by the absurd materialism or the absurd immaterialism that comes about when you don't take stock of the relationship between the living and the non-living. The dance is, in my

eyes, one of the most important sites of this relationship. It is no accident that a great many mystics use dance as prayer.

DD: That evokes the work of Edouard Boubat. In his photographs one perceives a kind of "solidarity" between the inert elements and the solitudes of the bodies. There is a Boubat photo of an old woman, really at the end of her life, resting on a bench near Saint Sulpice in Paris, and what's fantastic about this photo is that it gives you the impression that the street and the feet of the bench are supporting her, are in a strange rapport of solidarity with her, are sharing her solitude, accompanying her. That's why, when you spoke of nazism — of blood and soil — I was thinking that there was also a change in the light, a change in the register of the light, which transported a crowd of bodies: that was one of the vectors of what has been called the total mobilization. How can we invent systems of movement today that can create effects of solidarity between distinct bodies, of distinct morphologies, with distinct rhythms and dynamisms, but without necessarily producing in the end a mass effect in the totalitarian sense of the word?

PV: That's true, that's completely true,

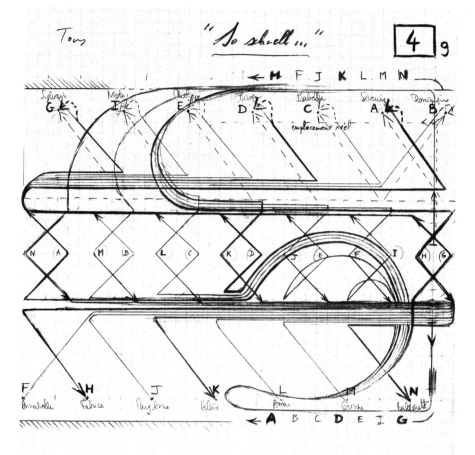

← H F J K L M N

Sylvain   Mola   Christine   Hervé   Isabelle   Séverine   Dominique
G   I   E   D   C   A   B

emplacement arrêt

N A M B L C K D J E F I H G

F   H   J   K   L   M   N
Annabelle   Fabrice   Delphine   Héloïse   Armand   Gisèle   Baldinette

← A B C D E I G

"So Schnell..."   Graphique d'ensemble : 9
14 mesures — de 69 à 82.

but it began with futurism. One mustn't forget what nazism took from fascism and what fascism took from futurism, so it's true that it all begins with futurism, but for them it's an assault. You find it again with Heidegger, but to make an assault on the world is not the same thing as falling into the world. Of course it is a movement, but its interpretation is completely different: to make an assault on the world is to exercise violence in the fall. With the Nazis the fall of the assault is a conquering fall, whereas with the chuteur à vue it's exactly the opposite: I risk death to gain the world, to acquire it. It's an acquisition of an objective, the parachutist who throws himself into the void wants to acquire the world through his weakness. It's an anti-assault.

DD: That's it, that's always the crucial question. So why is it that there is always a possible ambivalence between the moment where it could either be winning the world by my weakness, by my fall, or it could be the kamikaze dive which is the excess of that fall? Therefore the question, in choreography for example, is at what moment can I be practically sure that my fall is not going to be a kamikaze fall, but a fall to "win the world in weakness," to be on the side of

weakness, as Bram van Veld puts it? It is this difference which is at stake.

PV: Once again, I can't really answer because what I feel like saying is that human freedom is there, that is in a certain way the enigmatic liberty of living things. And there would be some important work to do on the notion of liberation, because I recall that with rockets there is a speed of liberation, an escape speed, which allows man to emancipate himself from gravity. In the example of the parachutist it is the opposite, he remains within the constraint of gravity and it is within this gravity that he acquires the world as the experience of the fall; thus he prefigures what could be a new perspective, he falls horizontally, he falls vertically, it's a fall toward the horizon and no longer towards the ground. We're touching on things without any answer, questions of freedom: you can choose the assault, you can choose suicide, you can choose grace, but it has to be a choice.

DD: Is it a choice or does something completely unpredictable and imponderable remain, which means that at a given moment you swing either toward the fall or toward grace?

PV: There is death. It is clear that today

21 ▶

with the bungy jumpers there is a suicidal dimension which leads back toward drugs, it's quite terrifying. So in a certain way, you can throw yourself into life just as you throw yourself into death, and that's one of the great differences between assault and flight. We just had an example of flight in Irak, it's a precipitation into life, whereas we could have seen the reverse, a precipitation into death. I can't say anything more about it, it's a problem of choice, everyone is free to choose death.

DD: His own death.

PV: Yes, his own death.

DD: But when one is suddenly led to choose the death of others?

PV: That gets us into another debate.

DD: There's a kind of disproportion...

PV: I think that when you choose the death of others you have already chosen your own, but you go about it another way. But I'm not a moralist.

DD: At the same time, there is a threshold where one would like to see these morbid or murderous things suspended. In the practice of dance and of choreography, there is one possibility given among others, the possibility of veering away...

PV: I'd like to offer an image: the difference between dance and the arts of combat. You can dance with pride and you can dance with modesty; for me the greatest dancers aren't proud. I've seen great dancers — I won't quote their names — who danced with such arrogance, with such pride, that although it was technically perfect, it was emotionally awful. What does it mean to fall with grace, if not to fall modestly, to fall into the world with humility? I would say that these great dancers I'm talking about and whom I find so awful are combatants, they have a way of spinning around like warriors, with warriors' gestures, like samurais, like certain combat sports, they have a force, an arrogance, a pride that makes them perfect but awful. I've often felt that in dance.

DD: Yet one often has the impression that people, and powers, like to see arrogance. They seem much more desirous of an occupation of space than a preoccupation with it. One has the impression that sometimes despite themselves, because they are subject to so many pressures, choreographers seek to take over space instead of preocccupying themselves with building it, inhabiting it, learning how to penetrate it according to its implicit rules.

PV: Once again I can't say much, except that I don't want to see any more of that kind of dance; for me it's completely out of date. I saw too much of it, in the fifties and sixties, after the marquis de Cuevas's ballets where I went regularly. I saw too many things like that. I found it dated quickly, it got terribly old: in a certain way it became a parody of dance. What interests me in contemporary dance is its inventiveness, its innovation, the fact that it's never the same, it's always different. From this point of view you can learn a lot from the dances on vertical walls.

LL: How do the traditional systems of representation function with respect to the living present? Semiotics supposes its absence in order to formulate the idea of the sign; but it could seem that we are working at cross-purposes now, because dance notation, for example, either tries to clear its territories — and when it approaches us, it is not a notation of territory — or on the contrary, it shows their entanglement, which will constitute itself as a fall, as a hollow space within a territory. How can this tracing constitute itself within the living present?

PV: That is the difference between the aesthetics of appearance and the aesthetics of disappearance. Despite their initial principle, many classical dances fit into the aesthetics of appearance: "Did I land well, did I keep the beat?" Today dance is rediscovering its principle, which means it is faithful to the aesthetics of disappearance. It shows movement all the better because the body is in flight, and falling. Thus it rejoins arts of representation like music, like cinema, it accepts the priority, the primary, of the aesthetics of disappearance over the aesthetics of appearance. Let me recall that persistence, in the aesthetics of appearance, is the persistence of matter, whereas in the aesthetics of disappearance, persistence is retinal, it the persistence of memory, of the mental image. I think there is a key period for this, which is that of French classicism; I won't speak of it in detail, I don't know it, but I've seen dances from this period, I mean lots of dances, where appearance is a very important element: it's enough to see the dancers' costumes to understand that they aren't at all evanescent, they are encumbering things. When you go from that epoch to our own, where the aesthetics of disappearance has the upper hand, then the body is naked, naked in the sense we were talking of a moment ago: a fall into appearance, or rather, a fall into transparency.

LIFE SCORES

Interview with Laurence Louppe

LL: Dancers take an interest in your ideas because you are one of the few people today who quite readily work with the interplay of the organic and the imaginary.

RT: That is a fitting definition.

LL: All thinking on the subject of dance and dance notation has in fact been confronted with this passage between the two, which can neither be accounted for intellectually, nor explained to others without difficulty.

RT: Yes, that's true. I mostly deal with this mixture of organic and imaginary elements from a strictly biological viewpoint. To my mind, it will never be possible to set up a rational theory of biological organization without combining both concrete and imagi-

nary elements. Unfortunately, modern science confines itself to the study of molecules, and neglects the world of the imaginary. I think that all modern science operates on a level which will never foster a point of view founded on any degree of synthesis. The position taken by dancers is a little different, however. I cannot claim to be a specialist in dance, for I have written only one article on the subject... I practically had to publish it at my own expense. The only reason for this article actually being published was the appearance of the large collection of articles called *Apologie du Logos* ("In Praise of the Logos"), and I am not sure my piece really deserved publication.

LL: In this article, there are a lot of elements which tie up with the preoccupations

◀ 22

61

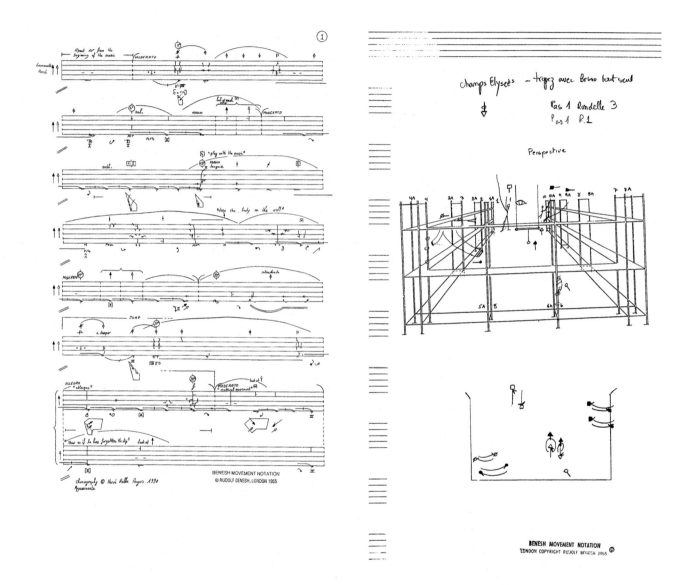

Champs Elysées — trapez avec Bruno tout seul

Pas 1 Rondelle 3
Pas 1 R.1

Perspective

BENESH MOVEMENT NOTATION
© RUDOLF BENESH, LONDON 1955

Choreography © Hervé Robbe Rogers 1990
Appassionata

of writers of notation, and in particular with the idea of generative fields, which you apply to the domain of choreography...

RT: I suppose that is not so original.

LL: It is not original in practice, but it is extremely original to find a thinker who is not involved in the practice of dance, yet who formulates such an idea. The idea of the generative field is extremely important.

RT: We can propose an initial model by considering each dancer as the molecule of a fluid; the dancers then create the dynamics of a continuous medium which one can consider as a liquid. One first has to face the task of defining the overall distortion brought into effect by the ensemble of dancers in the course of time, a distortion which involves either expansion, or contraction. In the case of expansion, the corps de ballet as a whole dilates towards a bigger space, whereas contraction entails the opposite process. The whole is therefore linked to singularities, fixed points which are retractive in the case of contraction, and repulsive in that of dilation. There also occur splits, resulting in secondary formations, where there is generally an additional use of the vertical. The most interesting task one could set oneself would be to study, again on the basis of the opposition between expansion and contraction, the rela-

tion of the movement of each dancer to the overall fluid, and to closely analyze the resulting interaction of states of concordance and discordance, both of which are equally feasible. It is necessary to construct a sort of topography of individual dance, by attributing an affective content, of repulsion or attraction for example, to each elementary gesture. Ideally, one should integrate the coloration emanating from each dancer's topology into his or her spatial displacement. The coloration would then appear as a local "derivative" (in the mathematical sense) of the dancer's spatial field[1]. Stylistic effects could, however, reverse this correspondence, in which case the artistic result would be quite surprising.

LL: Some notations, like those of Merce Cunningham, are based on aleatory processes. Here one merely draws out the pattern of elements which already exist. For example, one technique in dance composition involves holding up a sheet of paper to the light and reading a potential choreography from the imperfections visible in the texture of the page.

RT: This represents a physical basis for dance notation, a physical model whose variations could be interpreted in terms of choreographic figures. I was not aware that such things existed.

◀ 23

◀ 24

LL: This effectively ties up with an aesthetics of the pure concomitance of events, which are not interconnected by...

RT: ... by any law whatsoever...

LL: ... at least not by a law applied as a direct result of subjective intention.

RT: I feel that one should avoid confusing a dynamic process which could be compared, let's say, with someone who might shake a saucepan full of water, an action which would naturally send waves across the water's surface. In this hypothetical example, there clearly exists a generation of forms, but it is not stochastic in nature. It is constrained by the limits imposed on the rippling movement of the water by the movement of the hand holding the saucepan. It is impossible to move the hand freely in any direction, so there is a sort of organic constraint involved in the evolution of this form, a constraint one might be tempted to call aleatory, but which in reality is something quite different. It is, in fact, deterministic, more or less deterministic, that is. I cannot be sure... I would have to see the mechanisms employed by Merce Cunningham.

LL: But his idea has always been that his personal influence, taken as a subject, is less important than influence coming from outsi-

de. In other words, he would necessarily aim to renew existing forms, including psychological forms...

RT: Well, I would have to examine the functionning of his work in detail to really know. However, I do have the impression that a ballet or a choreography should nevertheless contain something resembling a unifying theme, even if it amounts to nothing more than a narrative theme, for example. Isn't this always the case in dance?

LL: No, a lot of choreographers already work on a theme which...

RT: In the beginning, dance was extremely ritualized, sacred etc... At this point, the things we are considering were organized into strictly coded structures. After all, couldn't it be said that there is a certain contradiction between the idea of dance, and that of freedom? Is it possible to dance freely, in your opinion?

LL: I think so.

RT: After all, the essence of collective dance involves an aim to achieve some kind of unity.

LL: Yes, in this case, the choreographic act and notation can be considered as limits imposed on freedom.

RT: Of course, all notation is principally a form of restraint, something which limits

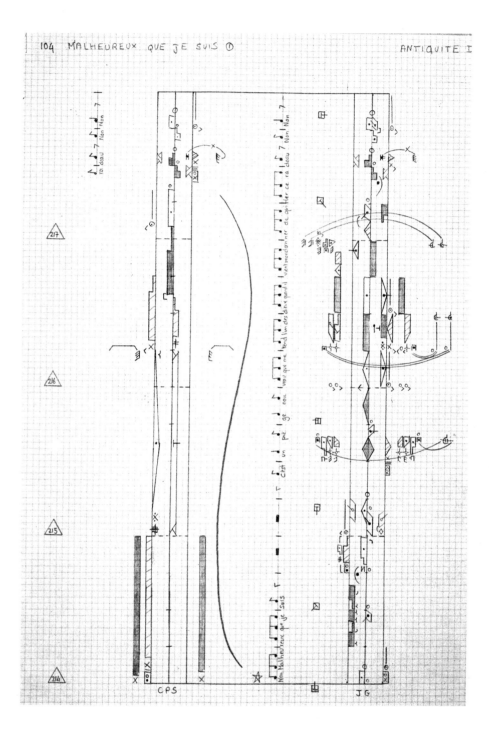

freedom, and this should not be a source of great surprise. Paul Valéry said that "Art thrives on constraint, and dies of freedom," and I think the same thing must apply to dance. Once restrictions become too diffuse, or once dancers are allowed to do as they please, I think nothing very interesting can be produced as a result, unless there has been some agreed arrangement made in advance, or something like that.

LL: You spoke a minute ago about the human body, its anatomy, embodying a form of constraint in itself, which you described in relation to the movements of water.

RT: The human body is certainly a constraint in its own right. It can't just do anything. I think that a large proportion of dance aesthetics must be concerned with the optimal ways of overcoming organic constraints, the constraints of bodily dynamics.

LL: I'm not sure how you would define corporeal constraints, whether you would consider them as belonging to the realms of anatomy, skeleton structure, psychology, or perhaps to that of the unconscious. In either case, the body is actually equipped with a built-in choreography, as it were.

27

RT: This is true, though this choreography remains implicit. Recently, while watching television one evening, I saw a program about circuses with absolutely amazing acrobats, performing oriental style gymnastics where they fling their backsides over their heads, which is something quite remarkable. The main factor in these performances is their inclination towards the extreme, for they push themselves to the extreme limit. "Extremity" effectively becomes the source of an aesthetic principle in these activities.

LL: In the case of acrobatics, I would agree, but in the case of dance, virtuosity is not necessarily a priority...

RT: So you think there is a difference between acrobatics and dance?

LL: Yes, most definitely.

RT: In what way do you sense this? How would you formulate this difference?

LL: I would say that acrobatics is characterized by different elements. On the one hand, there exists this confrontation with the extreme you were talking about, which doesn't exist in dance, because dance takes on elements which are purely qualitative as far as movement is concerned...

RT: Do you think that dance is purely qualitative?

LL: Yes.

Table de 12 noeuds premiers d'ordre inférieur ou égal à 7,
représentations graphiques des polynômes d'Alexandre.

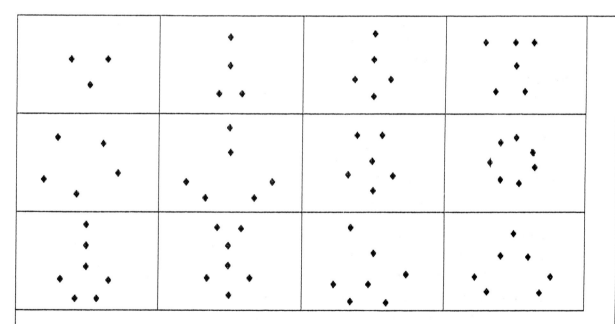

Table de 12 noeuds premiers d'ordre inférieur ou égal à 7,
représentations graphiques des polynômes d'Alexandre.

RT: So acrobatics must be quantitative, then.

LL: But the quantitative aspect can link up with...

RT: I always refer back to the example of William Tell, who shoots an arrow to hit an apple balanced on top of his son's head. This is clearly not acrobatics, but it can at least be considered an example of dexterity. The intention to hit the apple rather than the son's head constitutes a clearly quantitative factor, though this opposition is also highly qualitative, in such a way that there is a sort of quantitative constraint, motivated by very strong affective, qualitative factors. Does anything similar exist in dance?

LL: Of course, dance involves emotion, an affective content, both of which are essential factors.

RT: In dance, it is important not to step on your partner's feet, which is the least of constraints and probably passes almost unnoticed. There must be more to it than that however, though I can't define exactly what ... You say it is qualitative, which is one way of putting it...

LL: That is what can be observed at first sight. One could also point out that one's awareness of the body is not the same in dance. This especially applies to the center of gravity, for acrobatics always forces the body into an extreme position with respect to the center of gravity, by perpetually trying to contradict it, whereas dance allows weight to fall, retaining and controlling this weight if necessary, but nevertheless resisting any deformation of the gravitational axis.

RT: You mean that, in dance, the vertical of the center of gravity is maintained inside the support polygon traced by a given stance. Of course, this polygonal support varies... which is perhaps a good criterion for determining the opposition between acrobatics and dance.

LL: Acrobatics relies a lot on balance, whereas dance...

RT: Dance corresponds more closely to a controlled loss of balance.

LL: Exactly, controlled instability, a regaining of balance.

RT: Although it should be pointed out that even ordinary walking is a movement which periodically causes us to overstep our support polygon.

LL: In other words, we effectively set in motion a lateral exchange of supports. This is why Feuillet's notations from the seventeenth century, notations which you have seen, are essentially based on laterality, because the theory of baroque dance pre-

sents the lateral exchange of walking as the very foundation of all movement.

RT: In Feuillet's notation, the manner of positioning the feet plays the essential role...

LL: On the contrary, in Feuillet's notation, the stance is not the most important thing, and this is rather strange in itself. Feuillet shows one leg in isolation, parts of the body in suspension without any apparent point of support. The leg which is in contact with the ground, for example, is not shown. What is important here is the way the leg traces a central axis; each phenomenon is then divided laterally according to the shift of weight from one foot to the other. The most interesting notations of movement do not aim to recreate figures in order to show how movement operates in reality; they aim instead to recognize a center of movement and find a suitable means of notating it graphically.

RT: A sort of organizing principle which could serve as a basis for the whole configuration, and even act as an inspiration for this configuration, in both ways, both prior to and following the movement. This presents quite an interesting idea...

LL: Do you think dance could draw inspiration from the movement of animals?

RT: I think there are lots of analogies between the normal movement of human walking and certain movements of quadrupeds, at least insofar as vertebrate tetrapodes, as biologists would call them, are concerned. I have even come across a doctor in Versailles, Doctor Costagliola, who claimed that the movement of our arms as we walk is very similar to the synchronization of limbs during the standard walking motion of quadrupeds. So, the only exception is that there certainly is some dynamic continuity. Now, if you want to get into more complicated movements, like the dynamics of the fluttering of wings or the crawling of reptiles, the analogies will probably be more difficult to establish. No doubt, certain aspects of crawling and slithering may remain but they would have a marked expressivity. Those movements which somehow go beyond human norms and imitate typically animal behavior will certainly show a greater degree of expressivity, but they are more difficult to carry out... In spite of the advanced state of studies on the subject, I don't think that the problem of how to classify movements has been fully solved. It is taken on peacemeal according to the needs of the various discipline like people who study anatomy during a period of physical therapy. Technicians have a certain number of concepts at their disposal, but I believe that the general idea of a classification of movements and of the

organization of movements in relation to their intrinsical topology is something which goes beyond the average intellectual standard of a physiologist.

LL: Why?

RT: Because, by making a simple calculation, we can see that all the positions of the human body, the spatial positions of the human body that is, comprise a scope of about two hundred dimensions, two hundred parameters in all, if you count all the articulations... These parameters obviously include some which are important, others which are much less important. However, a systematic study of the scope of all the possible positions of the human body would involve taking into consideration a space containing two hundred dimensions, which is much too much for a clear, useful system of notation.

LL: You mean, in dance?

RT: Yes.

LL: There was Laban's system, however, which attempted to discern what he called 'scales,' as a means to link up the various possible positions.

RT: Did he make use of musical notation?

LL: No. Many did use the musical model in notation, but he didn't. 'Scales,' in this case, refer to all directions, whether high,

low, left, right, etc... encompassing the entire potential of human movement. I don't know if he actually brought together two hundred parameters, for what interested him most was rather the goal of determining the trajectories of dynamic forces, not their parameters. Parameters are of no interest to a dancer.

RT: Nevertheless, I'm still only referring to parameters; the movements taken within them would amount to something terribly complicated. A movement would then consist in a curve in this space of two hundred dimensions, something which, as such, would not be very useful. This would be characteristic of a mathematician's notation, abstract, and possessing universal validity but one which would clearly have no practical use, because it is humanly impossible to visualize more than three dimensions, or at the most four, for people who are in good practice, four being just about the absolute limit. Therefore, I tend to understand the problem of notation as being similar to the notation of languages of signs, a sign language. There not only exist sign languages for deaf people, for there are also forms of gestural language employed by some indigenous populations. Within the system of gestural symbols and the organization of gestures, one can perceive organizing principles

◄ 28

71

6th Couplet.

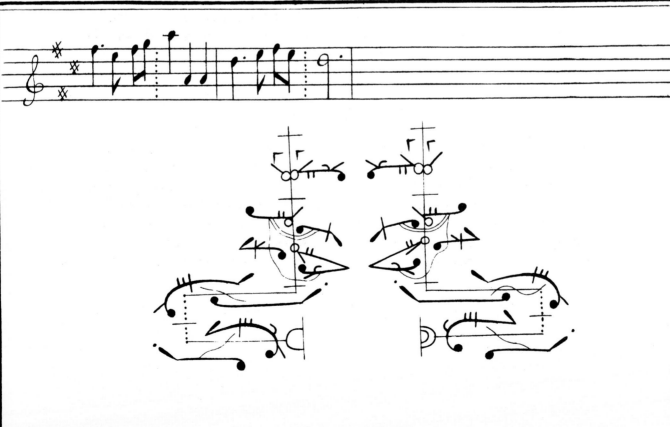

7th Couplet.

similar to those common to ordinary articulatory language, that is to say taxonomical principles like those found in biology. It would not be entirely impossible to set up a combinatorial analysis of elementary gestures, in the same way as linguistics facilitates the systematic analysis of varying combinations of phonemes in spoken language. However, something like this is not intrinsically plausible. In the case of dance, it would be rather unreasonable to suppose that there might be types of elementary movements fulfilling the same role as phonemes, or that all these movements could be composed of these elementary movements in the same way as a word is composed of letters.

LL: This type of thing did exist in certain types of notation, some of which sought to represent archetypal movements. In Laban's case, one finds what he calls the fundamentals, 'mother' forms, which do not resemble those you would normally look for, but which appear to be very interesting... I don't know whether you mean that there actually are semic forms or... Could not they be elementary movements of the human body? The first two basic principles of Laban are "I take, I throw," both of which are elementary movements of life. Some people also say "reach and pull."

RT: Yes, take and throw.. contract and dilate...

LL: These are the first basic principles. There are others, based on homo-laterality, etc... This verges on physical anthropology. However, I believe that your work in this field is breaking new, unexplored territory. The question I would like to ask you is, why you think it would be more reasonable to seek to establish these notations on the basis of a vocabulary made up of lexemes, units of vocabulary, rather than to find a universal mathematical pattern which could account for the two hundred dimensions you were just talking about. Which of the two types of notation would be more pertinent, in your opinion?

◄ 29

RT: Ideally, one should start with the universal mathematical pattern and then move on to observe and record things and, by examining the recordings, isolate portions of the process which possess great internal stability and which are frequently available for observation. This would result in "chreodes," obligatory paths, if I may borrow a term from Waddington which I use in my book. It is possible to imagine that, when we record movements, we are faced with systems which are relatively well determined in advance, movements which could be called "elementary chreodes." If we managed to isolate these movements as individual entities, and to then show to what extent they may depend on continuous parameters during the course of their evolution and their presentation, because of course every elementary chreode is also prone to vary... In a way, if you look how a skeleton is constructed, it is clear that it can be broken down into such component parts, for the mere awareness of the position of each joint between our bones permits us to reconstitute all the positions of the skeleton...

LL: All the possible positions of the skeleton...

RT: Yes, by establishing basic hypotheses, about the points of support on the ground for example, and if we know the position and angle of each joint, it becomes possible to reconstitute all the positions of the body. In some ways, this is a little simpler and easier to imagine than the space of two hundred dimensions I mentioned earlier, because the human body is organized along the lines of a genetic process. There are roughly two forms of relations. One is purely contiguous, an example of which is given when we say that the nose and eyes are situated close together. The other is a genetic relation, what I would call a "gradient," which leads from the center to the outer extremity, as when the embryo grows from the center outwards. By proceeding towards the extremity, for example, the hand develops as an extension of the arm, etc... The successive positions of the bones of limbs are therefore organized according to this gradient. The result is a structure in tree-form, after the fashion of the theory of graphs, which is canonical. The top of each of the structure's branches could be seen as representing the joints, and parametric angles, which together would constitute a certain type of schematization. Such a structure would naturally still belong to the domain of mathematics, although to a certain extent it does contain a degree of schematic organization, which biologists would describe as "centropetal." So, with the tree structure in place, it becomes possible to locate the positions of all the other parts of the body on the basis of the position of the trunk. Following this, it would be necessary to analyze the movements and try to classify them according to categories of the aforementioned "chreodes." In other words, every single joint harbors a certain "spatial configuration," if we were to put it in mechanical terms, a configuration which corresponds to all the angular positions which can be adopted by each joint. This space would involve 1 dimension for a simple joint, and 2 dimension for joints of the "head of the

74

humerus" kind etc... These are therefore local spaces with specific zones, which are generally subjected to frequent movement. Here again, it is possible to define "articulatory chreodes" and try to reconstruct movements from a sort of global dynamics, an articulation of elementary chreodes. It must be born in mind that this is only the outline of a program, so I don't know whether it would be tempting or even interesting to undertake this sort of thing from the practical viewpoint of the dancer. But in the abstract, it would have to be done like that.

LL: I would like to ask you if the two hundred parameters are not actually naturally inherent in the skeleton, i.e. whether the skeleton itself doesn't already contain a score.

RT: When I spoke of two hundred parameters, I meant that they are actually derived from the number of articulations. Among these, some are vital for movement, whereas others, like those connecting the middle joint and top joint of the fingers and toes, are almost entirely insignificant. The spatial dimension could be greatly reduced by restricting one's attention to the major joints, those which link limbs to the trunk etc., and those which determine the position of the hands...

LL: This would amount to what is called a "kinesphere," and be limited solely to the use of some of the simpler joints...

RT: Even just a small number of joints, like the scapular or the pelvic girdle, would enable us to trace the position of the body and the potential flexibility of the spinal column, though I suppose this would be quite minimal...

LL: You mentioned a progression in the construction of the body in embryonic processes, as you were talking about the crawling movement of reptiles earlier on... Are there some similar processes which can be traced back in human phylogeny?

RT: The isomorphism existing between embryonic development and phylogeny has been treated in the works of Haeckel-Muller, which draw us into a controversial field of biology. One aspect of his work in particular which has always surprised me is the problem of the embryology of functions. These are abstract entities, which are nonetheless characterized by a certain unity of biological operations which can often be easily spatialized, either in physical space, or in more abstract spaces like biochemical spaces... These functions favor a topological interpretation for spaces which contain both spatial position and internal biochemical activities.

I personally like to think that a function has a "soul." Functions are always somewhat cyclical. They end up at the point where they started by revolving around a fixed center, and this determines the soul of functions. However, this cyclical aspect of functions often slips from our memory, because it is generally said, for example, that the eye's "function" is to see, whereas in principle, seeing is not a circular function because light is taken in by the eye, but not given off. But, on the whole, such a circular plan is essential, and souls form the heart of cycles. However, this is a very abstract vision of physiology in general, and it is still far from being fully understood even by specialists.

LL: Such a vision is, to my mind, indispensable, inasmuch as we were talking about the quality of movement just now. Don't you think, however, that this quality could become apparent insofar as movement operates in liaison with function, and not only with the skeleton?

RT: Of course, but do you think that physiological, or what are more generally known as biological functions play a role in the organization of dance, for dance is, after all, a gratuitous action?

LL: Yes and no, it depends who you are. For a dancer, physiological functions are essential. The fundamentals of dance are expressed organically, not by means of language or symbols arranged into codes by the imagination. Around the time of the sixties in the United States, there was a whole range of basic research into deep muscle structure lying at the heart of the practice of dance, even though no amount of willpower could lay claim to, or control this structure. Such research was therefore more closely related to function than to motion.

RT: The notion of function in biology is, as you know, a very tricky notion. Everybody talks about it, though nobody knows what it is. I have always taken an interest in the question of the embryology of functions, and I have noted in particular that embryos only function as such once they have reached maturity. Its functions then truly function, whereas previously, during the intermediary period, function did not exist in full, for it too has to develop and undergo its own embryology. Some kinds of movement, like preliminary articulations, appear and ultimately organize themselves into a whole, embodying the biological end product, which is to say the preservation of the organism's overall balance. This intermediary process is very little known. What's more, given that the notion of function in general does not feature among the main

◀ 30

themes discussed by biologists, it becomes apparent that the embryology of functions is even less well known. This, however, is a different problem. Biologists are not dependent on theories in their work. Similarly, I think that dancers can also dance without theories, fortunately for them. Theoreticians are people who cannot do anything, and try to console themselves by other means as a result.

LL: I am not familiar with the situation in biology, but in dance it is difficult to construct theories without putting them into practice. Knowledge operates on the basis of experiences which are entirely practical.

RT: I am sure you are right.

LL: With respect to all the elements of the body you have been talking about, in what way does the body foster a meaningful relationship with space?

RT: If I were a Darwinian, I would reply by saying that a body which failed to maintain a meaningful relationship with space would be doomed to disappear quite swiftly. But I am not a Darwinian, and I find the question quite reasonable. Unfortunately, it can only be explained by saying that bodies do not stand in opposition to space, for space somehow constitutes an integral part of the construction of bodies. Biochemists try to convince us that this whole matter can be explained in terms of genes, which I consider to be a completely false assumption. Genes do play a role, of course, but they are not a fundamental aspect. On the contrary, the fundamental aspect lies in the spatial character of the formative process of the embryo, and this spatial character is permanent, because space is inevitably present from the start. If you consider this process from its beginnings, that is, from the sexual act, it starts off in the form of as an essentially spatial act. Space is present right from the start, and continues to exist all along, although life somehow infiltrates it and serves to organize space. You might well tell me that dance is merely the final stage of this explosion of life through the medium of bodily formation...

LL: Dance is often considered as an intrusion of the body into space...

RT: This is a profound philosophical question. By definition, a body is made of space. Aristotle said that "Things create space." Quantum mechanics also claims that each and every particle explodes, whereas modern physics, that of Einstein, claims the opposite, that space creates bodies. I would say that what you call the "kinesphere" is created in a state of "explosion" rather than a state of "intrusion."

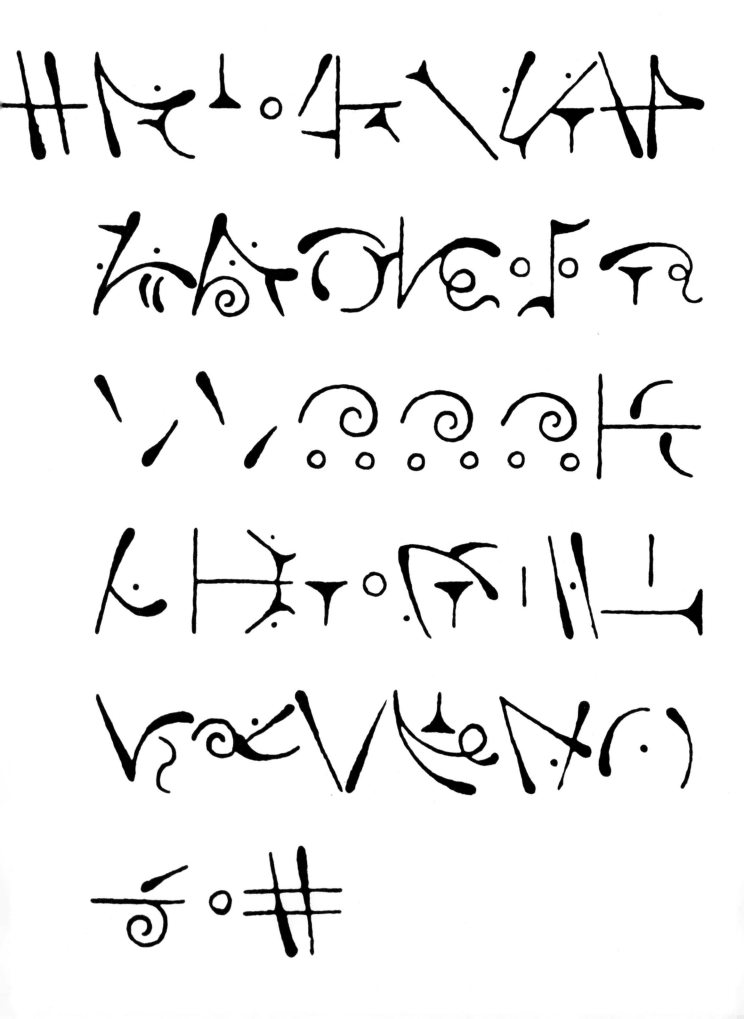

Neigungen der A-Skala

Punkt vh zu lz Neigung L9 (zlt)
» lz » hr » L10 (rhv)
» hr » vt » L11 (tvl)
» vt » rz » L12 (zrh)[1]

Eine räumlich gleichgeordnete Skala, in der die beiden in der Anmerkung erwähnten Schrägen vorkommen, ist folgende rechtsführend (B-Skala) von:

[1] Aus harmonischen Gründen, die wir später näher erörtern werden, *fehlt* in der rechtsführenden Skala die Schräge rhz — ltv, in der linksführenden Skala lhs — rtv.

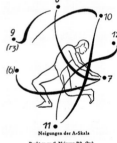

Neigungen der A-Skala

Punkt rz zu tl Neigung R0 (ltv)
» tl » vh » R8 (hvr)
» vh » lz » L9 (zlt)
» lz » tr » L0 (rtv)
» tr » sh » R5 (hsl)
» sh » vl » L6 (vlt)
» vl » zh » R ∞ (rhz)
» zh » zt » R2 (tzl)

31

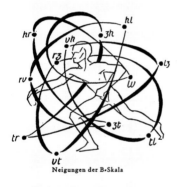

Neigungen der B-Skala

FEUILLET'S THINKING

In 1699, Raoul-Auger Feuillet published a treatise entitled *Chorégraphie ou l'art de décrire la danse, par caractères, figures et signes démonstratifs* (Choreography, or the art of describing dance with demonstrative characters, figures, and signs). The work is presented as the culmination of many years of research; at the same time, it marks the departure point for a host of subsequent publications that refer back to Feuillet's system for over a century, either to use it, to perfect it, or to criticize it.

◄ 32

Claiming the status of culmination, the book locates the origins of choreographic notation in Thoinot Arbeau's *Orchésographie*: proof that there was a sense of continuity from French Renaissance dances to the end of Louis XIV's reign, even if the lack of sufficiently numerous and precise documents makes it difficult for us to chart the evolution of dance across the seventeenth century. For, although the court ballets staged since the time of the *Ballet comique de la Reine* provided ample occasion for description, and although many drawings and engravings have been preserved, we do not possess (or at least, do not yet possess) any methodical technical texts in French for this period, excepting the *Apologie de la Danse* by De Lauze.

One may nonetheless remark certain attempts at choreographic notation. The most immediate consists in noting the "figure." This is what we observe in the description of the *Ballet de Monseigneur de Vendôme,* whose concluding section is

81

supposed to represent the alphabet of the ancient druids, "found some years ago in an old monument." Similarly, Father Ménestrier gives an account of the ballets he proposes as models by noting the positions of the dancers at the beginning and the end of their course[1]. Though integrated to Feuillet's more complete system, the principle of planimetric representation will continue to be used, alone and without any indication of the steps, for contredanses or dances in which the choreographer's interest extends only to the pattern of movement across the floor[2].

In between times, in 1661, Louis XIV had founded the Royal Academy of Dance, assigning it the mission of codifying French dance. For the royal power it was a question of replacing the privileges of the guilds — in this case those of the dancing masters and violin players — with a unifying organization, the artistic complement to the work of centralization and rationalization that ensued after the Fronde and, above all, after the assumption of power by Louis XIV[3]. It was also a question of imposing French influence, cultural and otherwise, on foreign nations.

33 ▶

To vehicle this official doctrine and the works in which it became manifest, the royal power and the dancing masters were inevitably led to reconsider the question of notation. It was in 1674 that Beauchamps received from the King the mission of devising an adequate system (or so it appears anyway, according to his own account[4]). The result was the treatise published by Feuillet, who was then brought before the King's Council by Beauchamps and accused of stealing the latter's ideas. Between 1674 and 1700, the Academy of Dance seems to have gone about its work in a somewhat disorganized fashion. In 1685, André Lorin had proposed a collection of contredanses noted in a system very different from the one developed by Feuillet (though it did use planimetric representation of movement across the floor); in Lorin's notation the steps were represented as units designated by symbols appealing primarily to abbreviations based on spoken language[5]. While exploring different pathways, the dancing masters must nonetheless have communicated the results of their work to one another, since the King's Council did in fact judge that Feuillet's treatise had grown out of Beauchamps' research.

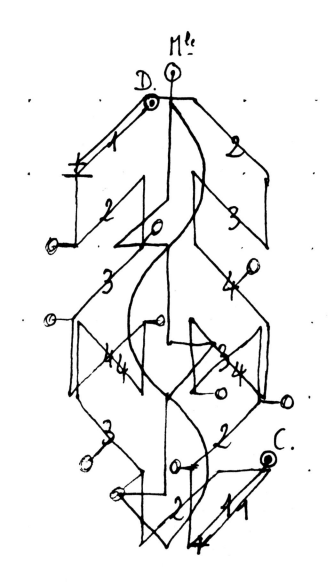

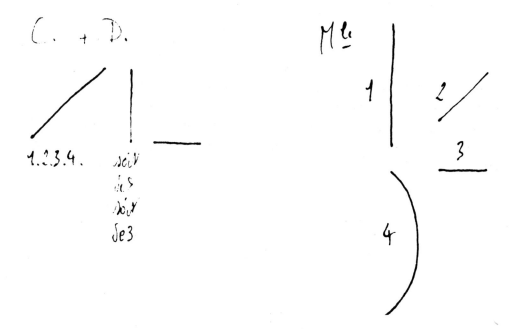

The question of notation was not definitively resolved by the publication of the *Chorégraphie:* in 1725, Pierre Rameau proposed to improve the system[6]. The aim of the modifications was, on the one hand, to avoid ambiguities and misreadings (by fleshing out, for example, the sign for a quarter turn), and on the other, to heighten precision by further developing the analytic representation of movement (explicitly representing which foot should carry out the rise or spring, in the contretemps or the march). This system ran up against violent opposition from the other dancing masters of the Academy[7], who mobilized against it both because they saw more disadvantages than advantages in changing the signs, and because they found Rameau's notation to be overloaded with information and difficult to read. The modifications were only accepted in Spain, where Rameau took up residence[8].

The Feuillet system would seem to have effectively fulfilled its goals, for it spread very rapidly. Numerous translations and adaptations of the *Chorégraphie* appeared abroad (two in the same year, 1706, by Siris and Weaver, in England alone). Feuillet's notation was also incorporated into systematic treatises describing steps (which Feuillet does not do): this is the case in Tomlinson's *The Art of Dancing*, and also in Dufort's *L'Arte del ballo nobile*[9], where each chapter closes with a square noting the step that has just been described. As to Feuillet's work itself, it was the object of numerous rewritings throughout the eighteenth century, with additions and updates to fit current tastes.

At the same time, Feuillet's writing allowed for the notation and publication of a great number of dances. The creations of the most famous French masters, Pécour above all, were made available throughout Europe (as demonstrated by Pécour's "Forlane pour femme," published by Feuillet in 1704 and reengraved by Pemberton in England[10], or by "Printemps," also preserved in an English edition); the system also helped to introduce the dances of foreign courts (here again, England shines by its contributions, mostly of ballroom dances, but also of pieces for the stage).

Alongside its use in dance collections destined for a widespread public, the Feuillet system served as an instrument for communication and elaboration within

...tan Murail...

C'est un jardin secret
solo alto
duo Catherine - Michel

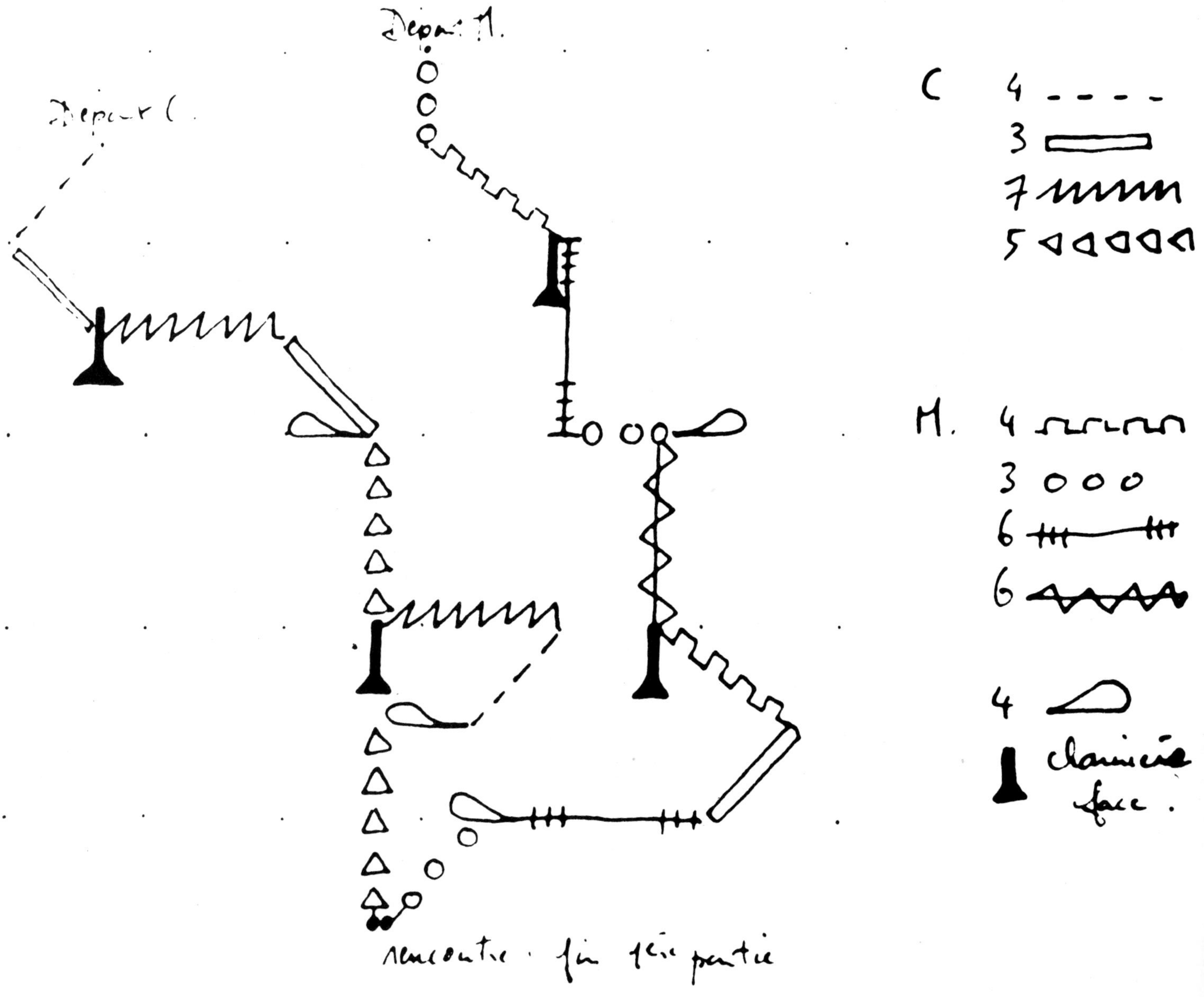

Départ M.

Départ C.

C 4 - - - - -
   3 ▭
   7 ⋀⋀⋀⋀⋀
   5 ◁◁◁◁◁

M. 4 ⌒⌒⌒⌒
    3 o o o
    6 ┼┼┼──┼┼┼
    6 ⋀⋁⋀⋁⋀⋁

    4 ◡
    ♟ clarinette
       face.

rencontre : fin 1ère partie

the milieu of the dancing masters. Where its status as a tool for communicating over a distance is concerned, one may cite, among other testimonies, the procedure detailed by a text from the Hardouin-Médor archive in Caen: the city's dancing masters are shut up in a room with paper, writing desk, "mathematics case, etc.," as if for a written examination; they compose choreographies for balls or ballets, which are then sent to Paris to be judged and classified by the Academy; only afterwards comes the practical test, or "execution." As to the role the Feuillet signs played as a working tool, it is established by the dossier *Rés. 817* of the library of the Paris Opera, in which several dances are noted in a cursive hand clearly intended for use within the professional milieu. This helps illuminate the testimony of Noverre[11], who ridicules the choreo-authors of his time for seeking their inspiration in "notebooks" where they have recorded the compositions of their predecessors.

Even though it was elevated to the rank of an institution, the Feuillet system never ceased to be criticized, and not only by those who reproached it for insufficient analysis, like Rameau. In parallel to the reworked version issued by Malpied[12], we find a polemic against it in the *Lettres sur la danse;* in Italy, Magri proclaims his ties to Noverre[13] and disdains any knowledge of Feuillet, going so far as to fabricate his own symbols for the notation of contredanses. Does this refusal of the system stem simply from the fact that dance, as Noverre says, had evolved since Beauchamps' time and become too complicated to fit into Feuillet's framework, particularly where rhythm was concerned? Noverre's text actually contains another objection, which he does not succeed in formulating clearly[14]: it is that Feuillet's writing, while detailing the succession of operations executed by the dancer's feet, does not account for the dynamics of the ensemble, for the "color"[15]. The same difficulty is found in musical notation, and indeed, in the notation of any discourse, above all a discourse charged with rhetorical force. How can the presence of the object be regained through that which decomposes it? How can a fluidity of movement be conjured by the immobile? This is the paradox explored in the seventeenth century, a period of cool formalism and intense passions (profane as well as religious); a century that claimed to "paint nature," that is, to give nature a new life by forcing it to pass through a code.

In effect, it is a truism to observe that Feuillet's system reposes on an analysis of movement extended further than ever before. Instead of considering the step as a whole, it specifies a sequence of elementary constituents. Thus the notation of an apparently quite simple and very dynamic contretemps balonné, with two "movements"[16], requires no less than eight indications: a step forward with the free leg, a sink, a spring, a foot in the air, a second sink and a spring on a half-position sign; the two groups of signs, corresponding to the two movements, are joined by a trait within the frame of the measure. And if this contretemps balonné were to be executed with a change in orientation, a supplementary sign would have to be added.

What is the explanation of such complication, against which so many novices rebelled? An historical reason can be invoked. The French dancing masters had to unify a vocabulary of steps with diverse origins, from the provinces or from abroad: to discover what this vast repertoire had in common, it was necessary to first distinguish all the constituent parts. This is what would permit the use of the same signs (in different sequences of course) to note down a minuet or passepied, originally from the west of France, as well as a gavot or a rigadoon, imported from the southeast, or a "Spanish-style" sarabande or chaconne. The Feuillet system thus reflects an approach which, by passing through the universal laws of movement, finally arrives at a kind of universal language of dance, allowing the different traditions to communicate.

Thus we glimpse another reason for the system's complication, theoretical and pedagogical this time: analysis permits one to highlight the function of each step in its rigor and its purity. In this respect, it is hard not to recall the second rule of the Cartesian method: "divide each of the difficulties... into as many parcels as you can, and as many as are necessary to better resolve them"[17]. Nor would comparison with the first rule be unthinkable: "... to include nothing more in my judgments but that which presents itself so clearly and so distinctly to my mind, that I have no occasion to cast it in doubt." Of course, one cannot ask a dance step to present the truthful character of a philosophical judgment, but it is at least certain that the constituents identified by Beauchamps and Feuillet, which form the object of a definition on the very first page of the *Chorégraphie,* are intended to be "clear" and "distinct"[18]. They are, in any case, much more clear and distinct than the totality of a step, which, despite its dynamic appearances, despite its material presence in practices emerging from a tradition, is nonetheless a complex object.

Once analyzed into its essential elements, this object could be reconstructed according to the third rule of the method: "to guide my thoughts in order, by beginning with the simplest objects and those most easily known, so as to rise little by little, as if by degrees, to the knowledge of the most composed..." It was thus, following the model of those "long chains of reasons, all simple and obvious, which geometers are accustomed to use, in order to carry out their most difficult demonstrations," that dance, or rather the explanation of dance, became a science, whose development is represented by the Feuillet system. The "characters" of the *Chorégraphie* are not only "demonstrative" because they show or indicate, but because that which they refer to has been clearly circumscribed and integrated into an order.

What does this strange science teach us? It teaches, first of all, what it was designed to: it teaches dancers, masters as well as students, to see clearly among the traditions which inform their practice; these traditions, forming something like empirical givens, are legitimated by this work which, after decomposing them, reconstructs them again, and, if necessary, even corrects them in points of detail, puts them back into order[19]. It also helps the dancer to know himself better, to grasp himself at each step in the functioning of his corporeal "machine." On the basis of fundamental operations, Feuillet's volume, a kind of *Treatise of the Passions* for the dancer's body, produces in the strict isolation of the squares that fill its pages the same steps that are otherwise known only in the unbroken flow of choreographic compositions.

But this does not exhaust the virtues of our strange science. Beginning with simple constituents, one arrives at the composed figures attested by everyday practice; but the development of the "long chains of reasons" can be pushed even further. Descartes claims that "as long you maintain the order necessary in order to...

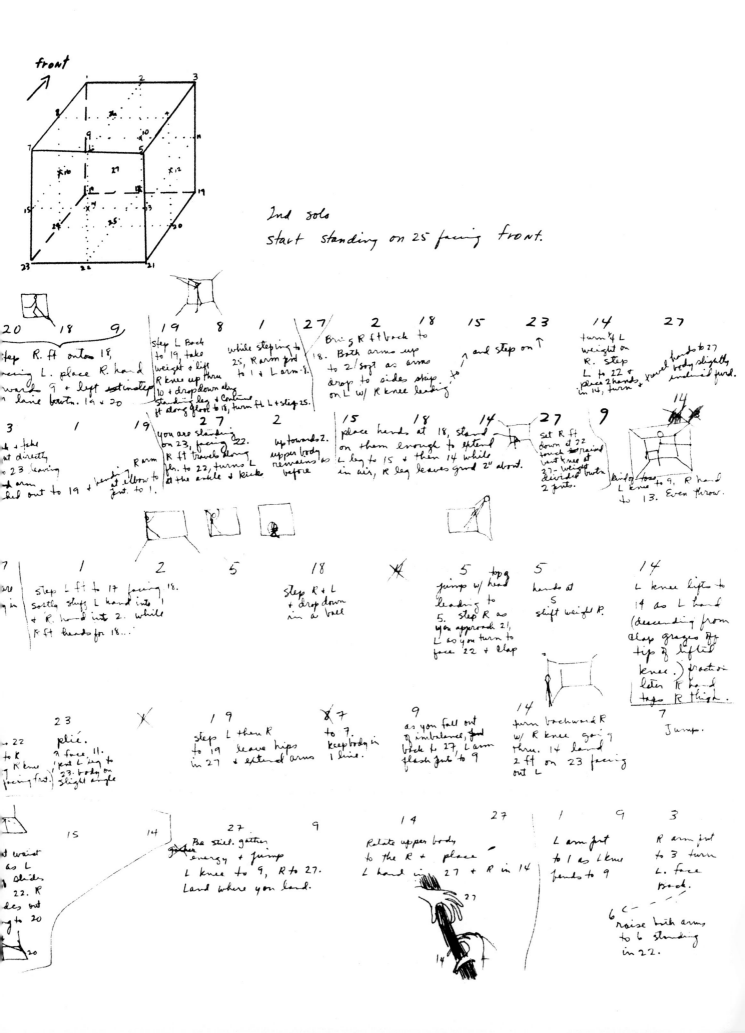

front

2nd solo
Start standing on 25 facing front.

20   18   9

Step R. ft onto 18, facing L. place R. hand towards 9 + left in instep in line between 19 + 20

3   1   19

... + take ... directly ... 23 leaving ... arm ... out to 19 + bending R arm at elbow to ft. to 1.

19   8   1   27

Step L Back to 19, take weight + lift R knee up thru 10 + drop down along standing leg + Continue ft along floor to 18, turn ft L + step 25. while stepping to 25, R arm prd to 1 + L arm 8.

2   18   15   23   14   27

Brig R ft back to 18. Both arms up to 2/soft as arms drop to sides skip on L w/ R knee leading to 1 and step on ↑ turn ¼ L weight on R. step L to 22 + place 2 hands in 14, turn. drwl body slightly inclined fwd.

19   27   2

you are standing on 23, facing 22. R ft travels along fl. to 22, turns L at the ankle + kicks R arm it prd. to 1. up towards 2. upper body remains as before

15   18   14   27   9

place hands at 18, stand on them enough to extend L leg to 15 + then 14 while in air, R leg leaves grnd 2" about. set R ft down at 22 touch raised rest knee at 27. weight divided both 2 pnts. Kind of toss L knee to 9, R hand to 13. Even throw.

7   1   2   5   18

step L ft to 17 facing 18. softly slips L hand into 1 + R hand into 2. while R ft heads for 18... step R + L + drop down in a ball

5   5   14

jump w/ head leading to 5. step R as you approach 21, L as you turn to face 22 + clap hands at S shift weight R. L knee lifts to 14 as L hand (descending from clap grazes by tip of lifted knee.) fraction later R hand taps R thigh.

23   plié.   19   7   9   14

...22 ... R knee ... facing fwd.) a face 11. post L leg to 23. body on slight angle step L then R to 19 leave hips in 27 + extend arms to 7 keep body in 1 line. as you fall out of imbalance, fall back to 27, L arm flash prd to 9 turn backward R w/ R knee going thru. 14 land 2 ft on 23 facing out L   7   Jump.

15   14   27   9   14   27   1   9   3

at waist as L slides 22. R ... des out ... to 20 Be still, gather energy + jump L knee to 9, R to 27. Land where you land. Rotate upper body to the R + place L hand in 27 + R in 14. L arm prd to 1 as L knee bends to 9 R arm prd to 3 turn L. face back.

6 ← raise both arms to 6 standing in 22.

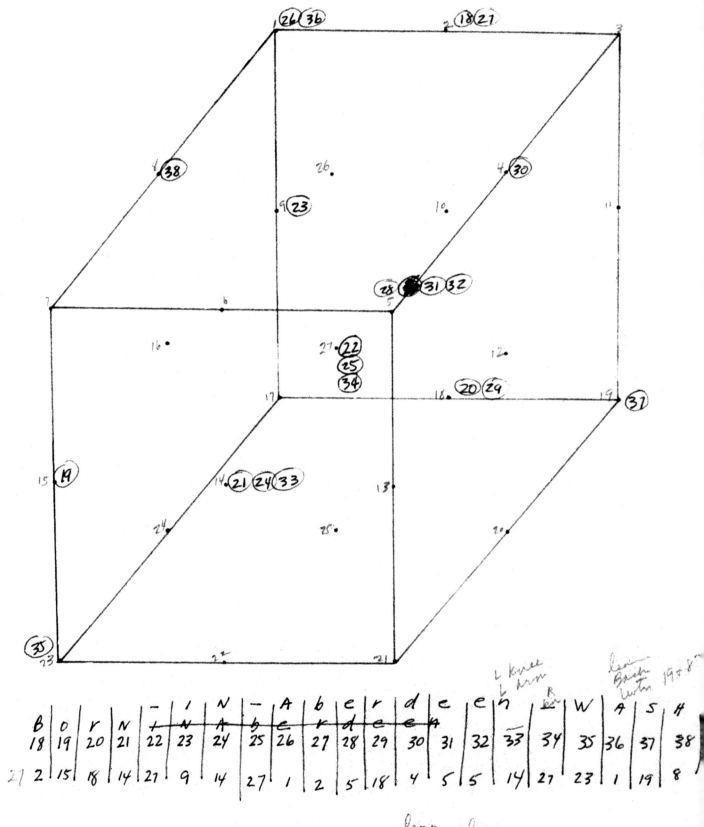

B	o	r	N	+	N	A	b	r	d	e	e	H					W	A	S	H
18	19	20	21	22	23	24	25	26	27	28	29	30	31	32	33	34	35	36	37	38
2	15	18	14	27	9	14	27	1	2	5	18	4	5	5	14	27	23	1	19	8

lexp clap
w/ head
going
thru 2
foot

deduce [the elements of knowledge] one from the other, there can be none you will not reach, nor any so hidden that it will not be discovered." The same hope may then be entertained for choreographic representation. "As long as you maintain the necessary order," that is to say, for example, as long as you refrain from immediate successions of two sinks, two rises, or two springs, you can form steps more complicated than those of the current repertoire. Thus the first movement of the contretemps balonné can be isolated and repeated, still on the same leg, while playing on the possible modifications in the course of the free leg: the latter, during the first spring, can beat behind, then in a second spring, beat in front, or describe a half-circle in the air; one may also add a half turn to each of the springs. One can also combine the beginning of a contretemps balonné with the end of a galliard, introducing a falling step[20]. It was in fact according to this procedure that each type of step, in the systematically progressing squares of the *Chorégraphie*, was adorned with beats, circulars, or changes in orientation; and the English pressed forward in the same spirit, rapidly inventing the sissone with contretemps or the gavot with contretemps in two "movements." Thus the vocabularies of the ball and above all of the ballet were enriched, by founding creation on the re-creation and exploitation of differences within the units of identity.

◀ 36

It would not be difficult to establish relations between dance and the culture of the century as a whole, just as we can link the institution of the Academy of Dance to the methodical organization of the kingdom in the political and economic spheres. For in classical French poetics as affirmed since the time of Malherbe, invention does not consist in an overabundance of basic elements: in the classical view, contrary to that of Renaissance humanism, the lived world in it its everyday presence has nothing exalting about it. For those who saw the horrors of the wars of religion, for those who saw the progressive triumph of a mathematico-mechanical model for the explanation of nature, it was out of the question that God should be present in the world, instilling it with his vitality; linguistic exuberance, which claimed to be an the emanation of this vitality, would henceforth seem part of an outdated ideal. Instead of entrusting artistic invention to the fantasia of fortune, it was now necessary to derive it from ingenious combinations of elementary units. This is the path of literary precio-

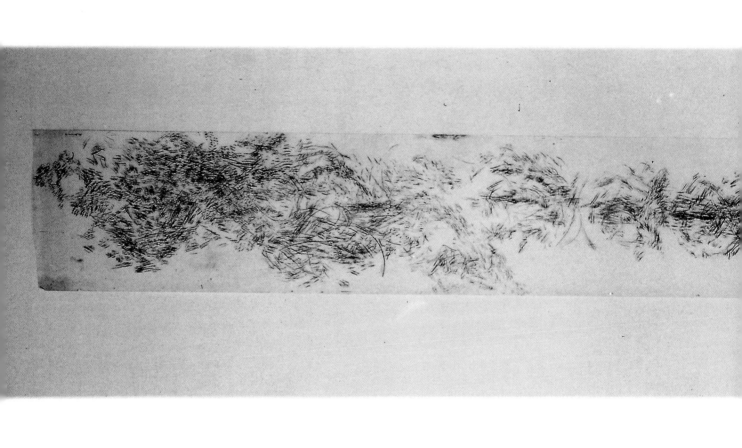

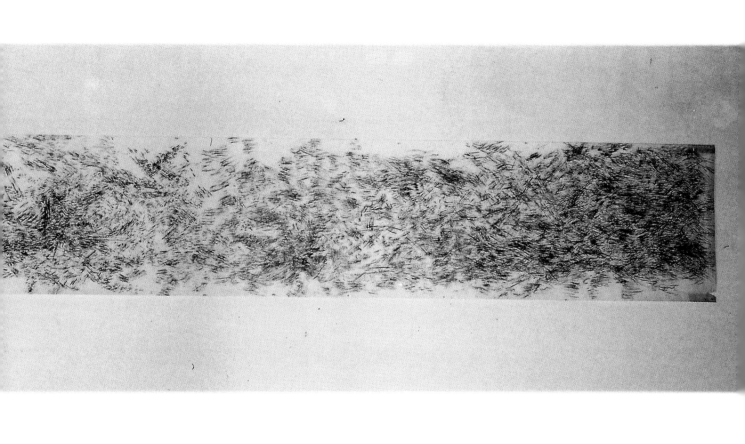

sity, extended by Racine and further pursued by the librettists of the lyric tragedies. Need we recall that such an approach, in its tendency to reduce the role of the immediate given, to quintessentialize it for the needs of a purely human combinatory system, is in no way a specific to the French seventeenth century? It is to the poets and scholars of Alexandria, so attentive to collation and concision, to analysis and rewriting, to displacements and ingenious superimpositions, that the period owes its doctrine of imitation; here, the delectable examples of Catullus and Virgil served as intermediaries[21]. This is not "imitation" in the Christian sense of the term (as when La Bruyère writes "everything has been said by the Ancients, and we can only pick over the shards," proof that human nature is irremediably fallen, miserable), but rather an imitation that takes up the limited character of the given elements as a challenge to the heuristic power of human method. And if one looks forward in time, it is clear enough how poetic work, understood by Valéry as research into the functioning of the intellect, could find its metaphorical complement in a dance that refers only to itself, which forms its own world and therefore can say, like Valéry's Jeune Parque:

◄ 37

"I saw myself see, sinuous, and gilded
From gaze to gaze my deep glades."

This is how the paradox of *fixing movement* will be resolved. Choreographic movement can only be fixed because analysis has allowed for the isolation of that which repeats in the multiplicity of occasions: a lexicon, an alphabet. At the same time, this fixed code can always be different, since each production arising from this language becomes a particular act of speech. Thus, just as spoken language cannot conceive speech as the pure emanation of the object which it designates, or of the subject who articulates it, so choreographic movement never presents itself as an irrepressible and immediate élan (or at least, it ceases this presentation at the very moment when poetic inspiration ends); instead it takes form in a system which only suggests a meaning after first passing through a network of internal relations, of "differences."

This principle, which organizes the language of choreography, will also organize its writing. Caught in this network of differences, the "characters" will become more "signs" than "figures." For if a concern to limit arbitrariness appears in the choice of the basic symbols, the construction of the system and the treatment of practical problems inevitably leads to conventions which, even though rationally deduced, nonetheless distance the signifier from the signified. Indeed, we must recognize that a large number of the elementary "characters" in Feuillet's system seem to refer quite directly to what they signify, either through their pictographic form, or through metaphor. Without even broaching the problem of the notation of the dancer's course across the floor (which, as we shall see, is equivocal), one can point to the stylized representation of the foot, the position, and the half position, as well as the notations of the step indicating the location of the ankle at the start (the "head of the step") and the orientation of the foot at the end. The category of metaphorical representations could include the "sinking" sign, set obliquely (sunk down) over the drawing of the step, in opposition to the "rising" sign, set straight; as for the "sliding" sign, one might hazard that the crossbar of the T represents the floor, with which the foot (the vertical of the T, perpendicular to the drawing of the step) remains in constant contact, whereas in the "falling" sign this floor symbol, symbolically cut in half, could represent the emptiness beneath a foot in the air[22]. In other cases, the conjectures become much more far-fetched, or even impossible, and one enters into the arbitrariness of the sign. But it is important above all to observe that the sign is generally motivated by the need to underscore the "differences." This explains the signs for "spring" and "caper": the spring being an amplification of the rise, it is logical to represent it by two bars, which, however, are in no way figurative; in the same way, the caper, which implies a more dynamic execution, is noted with three bars. Elsewhere the arbitrariness of the sign intervenes to dissipate ambiguities: one can consider the signs for "half turn" or "quarter turn" as figurative or metaphorical representations; but the fact that the sign "half quarter turn" is detached from the step constitutes a simple convention, destined to render the sign more readable[23].

To these elaborations must be added the distortion of the dancers' courses. The traces which represent them are interrupted by dotted lines when necessary, or are disproportionately lengthened to receive the indication of successive movements to be executed in the same spot: given the convention that represents both space and time on a single line, that of the dancer's path, an unforewarned reader could think that at the close of a given figure the dancers are at the far ends of the room, whereas the beginning of the next figure, which puts them back in their correct places, shows us one alongside the other. All of which means that a page of choreography, in its entirety, is no more the painting of a dance than a text is a direct image of its meaning (unless the text in question is a calligramme). That is also why the Feuillet writing can accept different forms of production and diverse degrees of calligraphy–engraving, manuscript copy, handwriting in detached or cursive characters[24]—without any alteration in the functioning of the system, just as there can be a wide range of variation in the way each pe rson shapes his letters. Thus we can go from Feuillet's soberly printed collections of dances from the years 1700-1708, to the calligraphy of Gaudrau's volumes, or of Roussau's in England[25], and then back to simple manuscript copies. The copy's finish no doubt tells us a great deal about the person who made it or had it made, but this type of information does not affect the code, which leaves no room for the spontaneity of the choreo-author or the copyist: everything must be elaborated, mediated[26]. To borrow an antithesis from Jean-Jacques Rousseau — one which sums up the opposition informing our romantic tradition — we can say that the language of Feuillet is a "geometer's tongue," not a "poet's tongue"[27].

What can this system express then? If the writing system refers back to a system of dance, two questions must be asked: to what degree of completion and exactitude does the notational system account for the act of the dancer which is supposedly being signified, and even more importantly, to what extent does the language incarnated by the dancer's act refer to anything outside choreographic semiotics? In short, is there a semantics of dance, whose content would be hidden in Feuillet's notation? Literary language sometimes comes to the aid of a researcher short on interpretation; and yet the information it delivers in turn gives rise to still more questions.

Textual sources remind us first of all of the difference between ballroom dances and ballets, and warn us not to look for any meaning in the former: it is frequently

repeated that ballroom dance is only a succession of pretty poses and must always be sweet and moderate, while stage dances are lively and figurative[28].

But precisely because ballroom dance was practiced primarily in the context of court ceremonial, in which princes, high nobles, and courtiers gravitated around the king like the planets around the sun, researchers have been tempted to ask whether the figures traced by these dances (which form their essence, since little complexity was sought in the steps) did not refer, in their very gratuitousness, to some cosmic or mystic meaning. Indeed, it is known that there existed in Italy a neo-Platonic tradition in which the figures of the dance, as representations of ideal mathematical relationships, were held to establish a link between the earthly realm and the divinity. What had become of this tradition at the close of the seventeenth century? And more generally, can dance be invested with a symbolic and esoteric meaning?

If one seeks an earlier reference point, it would be tempting to claim that in 1610 esotericism had official residence rights in courtly ballet, as the reference to the "druidic alphabet" in the *Ballet de Monseigneur de Vendôme* seems to prove. However, Margaret McGowan has shown how many elements in this ballet signal a shift in outlook toward political allegory and burlesque, that is to say, toward essentially terrestrial perspectives, a trend which increases, she believes, over the course of the century[29]. What is more, the druidic alphabet spoken of here is rather enigmatic: it could easily be no more than a gallant allusion to the pastoral novel *l'Astrée*, then in the midst of publication[30], and thus a simple matter of fashion, rather than a metaphysical conviction.

Historically, in any case, it is improbable that esotericism could have had an official place (even an implicit one) at the court of Louis XIV. Where religion is concerned, the king's aversion to any divergence from the Catholic path of mediation between God and man is well known: his opposition to quietism, which minimized the importance of the Church and the methodical observance of its rites, is characteristic in this regard. In addition, the Affair of the Poisons had the effect of criminalizing anything that had even the slightest connection to occultism. Under these conditions it is hard to see how the masters of the Royal Academy of Dance, a direct emanation of royal power, could have allowed themselves esoteric allusions in their compositions. At best one might say, with a certain plausibility, that they prolong esoteric traditions which they exploit through modification or combination, but whose original meaning escapes them.

Had they wished to introduce symbolic representations, alchemical figures for example, they would first of all have required an audience. But contemporary fashion seems to have taken another turn. Thus in the alchemical domain, when Thomas Corneille, Donneau de Visé, and Marc-Antoine Charpentier made a bid to go on mining the vein of tragedy — and of comedy-ballet — that had proved so rich with *Circe* and *The Unknown,* their 1681 production of *The Philosopher's Stone* ended up a failure[31]. This could seem surprising, given the public's enthusiasm for the theme of the marvelous, which flourished in the stage productions of the time, and especially in the Opera. Is there a contradiction here? No, because the late seventeenth century version of the marvelous, filtered through a precious novelistic tradition which had long since been purged of all initiatory resonances, mobilizes only pagan references. Clearly codified, this marvelous world of theater and dance is catalogued as fiction[32]; as such, it is a pleasant amusement. The various forms of occultism and esotericism, on the other hand, are linked to the Christian marvelous, for they involve the soul, demand belief, and bring a metaphysical perspective into play. But in fact, the official version of the marvelous, the pagan marvelous that flourishes in the gardens of Versailles, is no longer the magic sign that invites the soul to fly free of its mortal envelope. With the help of mythology's anthropomorphic representations, the inhabitants of the heavens have been domesticated on earth for the amusement of the new gods: is the rising Sun not fixed in a fountain pool, and does he not retire with his horses, at dusk, behind the ironwork gates of the grotto of Thetis?

The emptying of the heavens will bring on two possible consequences: one is the search for the true God, henceforth absent from nature, withdrawn behind this machine that is the world; the other is the systematic exploration of the physical realm, and notably of the corporeal and intellectual potential of man. Tragic thought incarnates the first consequence, ballroom dance shares in the development of the second[33].

39

For when an aristocracy claiming to represent a particularly perfect type of humanity begins to enact the ceremonies of the court as a performance staged for its own benefit and for the rest of the world, the ball then becomes one of the domains in which this more perfect humanity consecrates its mastery: not only over the body, but also over more conceptual objects, through the modeling of movement and the organization of space. Thus man grasps himself as the producer of these geometric figures: detached from all transcendence, they involve nothing outside himself. This mastery extends equally, no doubt, to social relationships, represented through the spatial relations between the partners, and between each individual or each couple and the public. For the directions, and above all the changes in orientation, are at least as important as the drawing traced by the dance; the turnabouts in orientation lend themselves very well to psychological interpretation, for example when the partners face each other for an enchaînement, then spin back to back, or draw away and then approach again, imaging break-ups and reconciliations, now with each other, now with the public.

Such dramas, however, exist only as potentials, at the level of suggestion, for ballroom dances must be moderate; they cannot be compared with the play of the mimic, as they claim to express nothing. Outside of any stage context, they explore possibilities; thus they are termed *danses d'exercice* [34], just as Valéry (once more) called the *Jeune Parque* an "exercise."

It would appear to be stage dance which incarnates meaning as act. All the theorists insist on its figurative character. But at regular intervals, from Ménestrier to Noverre, this insistence takes on the tone of a call to order, thus testifying that the choreo-authors were also tempted to make the stage into an exercise ground, the site of a more intense but still gratuitous exploitation of the virtualities of bodies and of space. Pure dance or figurative dance: to what extent do the choreographies preserved in Feuillet writing fit into one category or the other? Or rather, what means do we have to figure out the implicit references which, for us, are hidden behind every choreographic text?

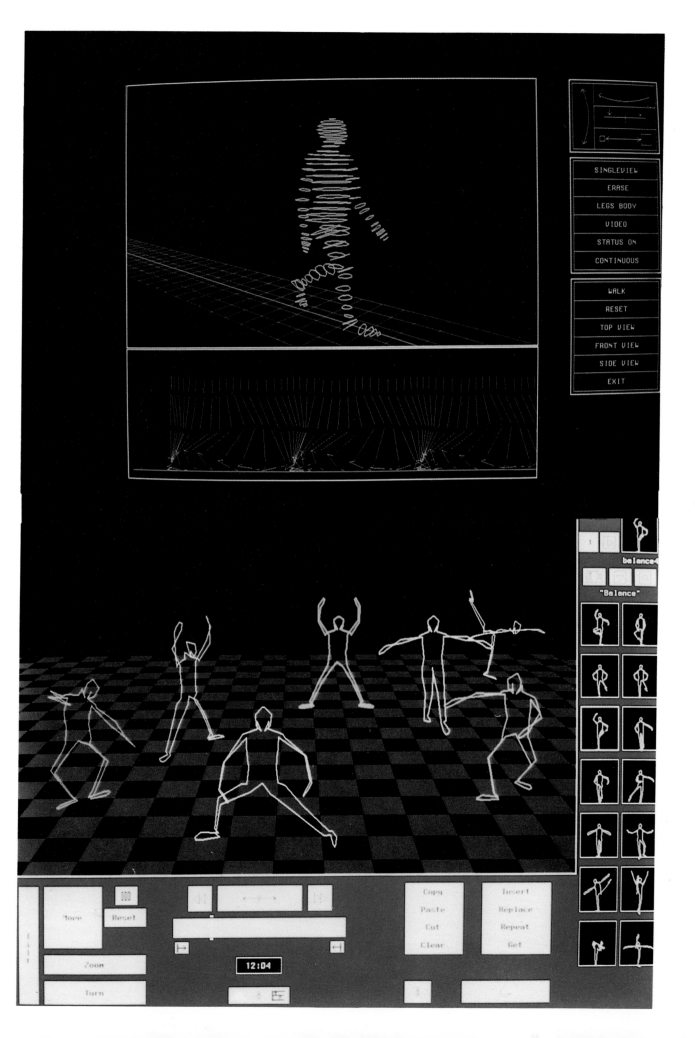

40

K.T. inv.   G. Bickham Sculp.

To James Stanley *Esqr. Son & Heir to* Sr. Edward Stanley *Bart. & to my much respected Scholar*
Miss Elizabeth Stanley *his Sister.*
This PLATE *is humbly inscribed by Their most obliged servt. Kellom Tomlinson.*

The indications that we read can leave the researcher rather perplexed. First, one observes extremely frequent discrepancies between the titles of the dances and the information given in the librettos or in the original scores of the operas. All that remains from the famous sarabande for Spanish men, in Molière's *Bourgeois Gentilhomme*, are choreographies for soloists, of which two are for women. In general, excepting Feuillet's *Ballet for Nine Dancers*, the ballet troupe disappears from the choreographies: the chaconne of *Phaéton*, "including troupes of Egyptians, Ethiopians, and Indians, male and female," becomes, in the various cases, a chaconne for a single woman or man[35]. This could be taken as a sign of the transformation of dance since the time of Lully and Beauchamps, Pécour's generation tending to privilege the soloist[36,] and Pécour himself having rewritten the choreographies and modified the distributions of roles. But the difficulty still remains when we see that the piece entitled "Air des Polinichelles" (Air of the Buffoons) in the score of the *Fêtes Vénitiennes*, choreographed immediately after its creation by Pécour, becomes "Entrée for Two Women" in Gaudrau's collection!

Leaving behind the question of the distribution of roles, we can also ask whether the text of the choreographies supplies us with precise indications about the expressive nature of the dances, indications which would correlate with the kinds of clearly typified characters we find in the drawings and engravings of the seventeenth and eighteenth centuries. Here again, and much more so than in musical scores, the clues are scanty. Beyond such notes as "Spaniard's Entrée," "Peasant's Entrée," "Pastorale," "Harlequin's Chaconne," etc., the dances are in no way situated in the work from which their music has been excerpted. Although the names of the dancers are often supplied, we are almost never told what type of character they are supposed to represent, nor in what dramatic context they intervene. Must one simply conclude that all these operas were so clear in the readers' memories that there was no need to recall them? For example, without even dwelling on the exclusion of all the "attendants" who are supposed to accompany the soloists on the stage, what explains the separate treatment, one for a man, one for a woman, of the sarabande and the jig of *Polyxène et Pyrrhus* in the dossier *Rés. 817* of the Opera library, when in the actual opera the two pieces follow one upon the other within a divertissement?

◄ 41

Why has even the indication "Tenderly" disappeared from the choreography, when it is noted on the score of the sarabande? ◀ 42 Why is this dance so clearly related to the "Spanish loure" type? Why, on a scale of relative difficulty, is the jig so much less demanding than what is normally required of dances for men? In short, are we really to see these two pieces as parts of a single sequence (which would imply an interpretation of their differences, of their resemblances, and of the seeming paradoxes they propose)? Or must we resign ourselves to seeing them only as isolated exercises, detached from their context? And if the second choice is the better one, would it also hold for a large number of published choreographies, including those of Pécour?

The only hope of answering these questions is to risk an interpretation of the expressive character of the stage dances (at least, whenever the dramatic context makes it seem that they must be expressive), and to see if they can be reconstructed along those lines. But here one comes up against the insufficiencies of the writing system: in particular, its failure to indicate arm movements. The only notable exception is found in the three choreographies that we have of Harlequin's chaconnes, yet in this case recourse to drawing and spoken language proves necessary. The notational system that Feuillet himself proposed for the arms, and of which an example is given for sixteen measures of the *Folies d'Espagne*, was never used in practice; in any case, it seems only to have codified highly abstract movements which, in themselves, barely show any agreement with the drawings that we have of ballet characters representing, for example, sorcerers or warriors. Reconstruction therefore entails a great deal of conjecture. This is the insufficiency which caused a great many people, long before Noverre, to deny the ability of the Feuillet writing to record stage dances[37]. This is why Noverre proposed to redeem the Feuillet notation by complementing it with drawing. Unfortunately, drawing only furnishes fragmentary points of reference: witness Lambranzi's engravings, which, despite the interest they present, finally whet our appetite more than they actually sate it.

In the absence of other indications, the notation of a contretemps with circulars danced to a hellish air resembles nothing so much the notation of a contretemps with circulars danced to a tender sarabande. Unless we resign ourselves to seeing the ballet of the early eighteenth century as the wholly inexpressive art described by ◀ 43

The 1.st Movem.t of the Chaconne ———— or Passacaille Step ended

K.T. Inv.t   H. Fletcher sculp.

To my ever respected Scholar Thomas Greasley Esq; Son and Heir to Sir Thomas Greasley
of Dracklow in the County of DERBY Bar.t and to his Brother, this PLATE is most humbly
inscribed by their much obliged Servant Kellom Tomlinson

Noverre, we must suppose that current practices allowed the reader to fill in the answers to questions that we ask today, and before which the choreographic texts remain so mute. This supposition would render somewhat more plausible the previously mentioned proposal of the Caen text, which has Parisian dancing masters judging, at a distance, choreographies of which a good many, according to the list that is given, are destined for the stage.

That certain things should be left implicit in the notational system comes as no surprise: everyone is familiar with the limitations of alphabetical notation, which are only partially overcome, by not entirely suppressed, by the international phonetic alphabet. The same imprecision intervenes in musical notation; and even the French, so fond of exactitude in general, and particularly when it is a question of ornaments or of measure, are quick to underscore the limits of their efforts. A composer as rigorous as François Couperin will write: "Just as there is a great distance between grammar and declamation, so is there also an infinite one between tablature and good playing"[38]. Thus we are forewarned: notation only gives us an outline, which we must interpret by filling in the gaps. No doubt this approach is only possible if we are familiar with what is tacitly understood; it is this familiarity, among others, that musicians call "taste," a notion which is of so little help to we who seek to revive practices whose living tradition has largely been lost. As François Couperin reminds us, a great deal was also left unsaid in literary language. One can cite Molière's well-known note to the reader, in which he advises that his *Amour Médecin* only be read "to people who have eyes to discover, in the text, all the acting of the theater." And recent research into the rhetoric of the seventeenth and eighteenth centuries, especially in its relation to the art of singing, have shown that detail by detail, every text destined to be spoken in public suggested emotions to be communicated through pronunciation, rhythm, intonation, and gesture, according to far more subtle procedures than the written code, procedures which at times could scarcely be formulated, but which, it was thought, could not be neglected without robbing the text of its effectiveness.

Where Feuillet's writing is concerned, can we rediscover the implicit content that would permit its effects to exceed what it literally says? In their respective fields, ins-

◀44

trumentalists, singers, and actors have been working on this type of question for a long time, obtaining specific results and sometimes very good ones. They know, of course, that their "reconstitutions" necessarily involve a degree of conjecture, and that 1990 can never be 1680. But by studying the corpus at one's disposal, both of works and of theoretical texts, and by considering each art in its relations with its neighbors, one can at least reconstruct a coherency, which translates, before an audience, into a presence. This type of work can be attempted systematically for dance. The first thing this entails is the regrouping of all the different orders of information that the documents of the time can give. It also entails the exploration (in statistical terms, for example) of the syntax of what is called "baroque" dance, and the determination of the constants and variants between the choreo-authors, between the various types of dances, between a given choreography and another, etc. This exploration of the internal coherency of the corpus of works is complemented by confrontation with the music; and a confrontation with the context given in the librettos is also called for, involving conjectural research into what may have been figured by the dance (and accepting that the single answer must often give way to the plural). On the basis of these givens, including some that must be accepted as working hypotheses, one can hope to reduce the proportion of that which cannot be recognized as figurative and thus must be classed until further notice in the domain of pure dance, of the "exercise." Through this exploration, one could ultimately hope to isolate a choreographic rhetoric that would henceforth allow the texts to answer our questions.

Thus the Feuillet system, seemingly so clear and exact, actually calls for a vast program of research. We have seen that it reflected the century's evolution, which tended to give human reason the power not only to interpret the world, but to rewrite it. Will art be reduced to the pure development of this reason, which would have nothing left to contemplate but itself? Or will it provide grist for reason's mill, in the forms of passions of the soul and of what is called life, the stage being one of the places where language-centered reason brings life back within its deeper order? At the crossroads of two centuries, is Feuillet's writing only the reflection of a long gaze at the tranquility of the gods? Or does it dare to drink the water that gushes forth from the stone? Research, perhaps, will tell us.

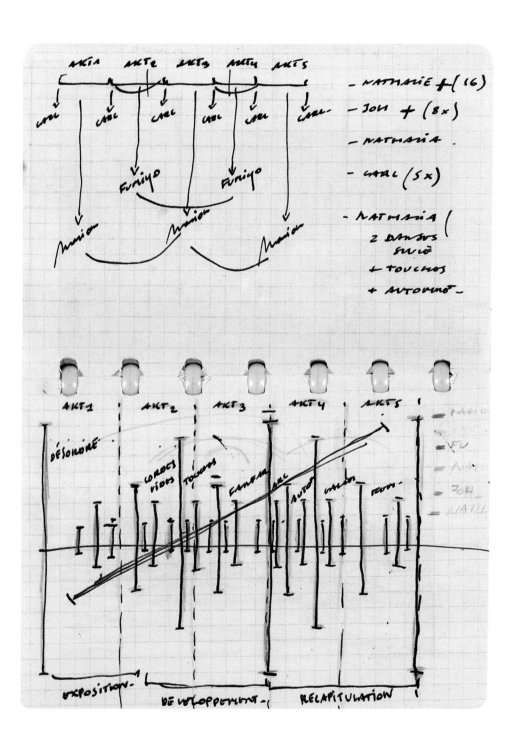

LABAN, SCHOENBERG, KANDINSKY
1899-1938

The innovative work of Laban, Schoenberg, and Kandinsky has had profound effects on the worlds of modern dance, music, and painting. The interest of a comparative study lies in the way these three artist/researchers crossed paths, the influence of the cities where they lived, and their highly individual, yet still complementary responses to the *Zeitgeist* of early twentieth-century Europe. The period covered here is from 1899 to 1938, focusing on the intensely creative years of 1908-28. In considering the interrelationship of the three men I will give special emphasis to Laban, for the lives and work of Kandinsky and Schoenberg have been excellently documented, while scholarly consideration of Laban is only now being undertaken.

Their separate beginnings. Rudolf von Laban, Hungarian by birth (1879) but Austro-Hungarian by upbringing, lived in Paris as a bohemian art student from 1900 until 1907, supported by an allowance from his family. His initial artistic ambitions were in architecture, which he studied somewhat erratically at the Ecole des Beaux-Arts. He was already trying abstract oil paintings, and also figurative illustrations. His activities included participation in the cabaret scene where he worked as a caricaturist, both in graphics and on the stage. His intention to devote his life to dance was not yet evident, but he did begin to study posture and behavior for his painting career.

Wassily Kandinsky, Russian by birth (1866) and upbringing, commenced the study of law and economics at the age of twenty. Having encountered art in Moscow and on visits to Paris, and opera at the Bolshoi, he eventually left for Munich, aged thirty, to study painting. He was free of financial anxieties.

Arnold Schoenberg's home base was Vienna. Born there of a merchant father, he attended the Realschule, receiving his first music lessons from his much-admired teacher Oskar Adler, and later privately from Alexander von Zemlinsky, a teacher at the Conservatory. He had no formal education in composition, starting to compose as a natural part of amateur music-making. His intention to be a composer only gradually developed. By 1900 he had written a first sketch of *Gurrelieder* but, with no money behind him, he was unable to devote his time to composing and worked as a "hack" orchestrator. In 1901, aged twenty-seven, he married Zemlinsky's sister and in an attempt to provide a reasonable living moved to Berlin as conductor of a Parisian-style cabaret, the "Überbrettl."

Laban and Schoenberg in Vienna, Paris, and Berlin. Already the scene was set for the interrelationship of Laban and Schoenberg to begin. It was based in their common Viennese heritage.

An important aspect of the urban culture shared by Laban and Schoenberg was Vienna's Art Nouveau movement — the "Secession" — and the associated architectural and craft fraternity. Laban's extant drawings coming from the 1912-14 period are Secession-style drawings. The elongated lines of Klimt, the eroticism of both Klimt and Egon Schiele can be seen in Laban's graphic work. However, Laban was never personally part of the Secession circle of artists, while Schoenberg did enter into its fringes, especially through his friendship with the architect Adolf Loos and the painter Oskar Kokoshka. Schoenberg was an active participator in the café life of Vienna, especially Café Museum and Café Herrenhof. The writer Else Lasker-Schuler, also a habituée of the café scene, is a possible connection between Laban and Schoenberg. Could Else have known Laban in Vienna at this period? Some years later she went to Monte Verità's summer seasons and there became intimate with Laban and his

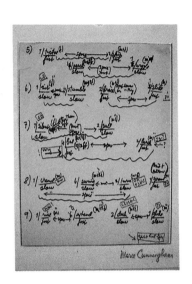

"star" pupil Marie Wiegmann[1]. Laban's summer seasons in 1913, 1914, and 1917 ◀ 46 were spent at the colony where an alternative life style in tune with nature was fostered. Here he opened his School for the Arts and promoted the practice of movement for all the colony, centered around his own group of dedicated young dance pioneers.

Laban saw Kokoshka's play *Morder Hoffnung der Frauen* in 1909, a vanguard multi-media performance which ended in a near-riot in the city's streets. The theme, the relationship between the sexes, was of intense topical interest because of the newly found confidence and free living of the emergent emancipated woman. Laban, for whom women were equal to men as companions and co-artists, found that Kokoshka's play stimulated his own convictions. Schoenberg deals with a similar theme in his later "Gesamtkunstwerk" experiment *Die Glückliche Hand* (The Lucky Hand) but his close friend Karl Kraus, the editor/owner of the socially conscious magazine *Die Fackel*, thought otherwise: "Women experience and men think" was his view. The intellectual woman was anathema to him.

When Schoenberg worked at the Überbrettl cabaret in Berlin (1901) he encountered an environment familiar to Laban. This kind of cabaret was brought to Berlin by Baron Ernst von Wolzogen and followed, in the main, the Parisian pattern of the cabarets in Montmartre and the Latin Quarter (Laban's studio was in the Boulevard Montparnasse). The political satire of the French would never have been tolerated by the Berlin censors, and the Parisian habit of allowing amateurs to recite their own poems and sing their songs was likewise dropped, as the Berliners had no talent for that kind of activity. Otherwise the cabaret was French in nature and immediately a success. Schoenberg conducted songs, dances, and incidental music for eighteen months.

Like all experiences, the cabaret activity remained part of the work of both Laban and Schoenberg. In Laban's case his natural gift for satire and the grotesque was fueled by his cabaret experiences, and appeared in many chamber dance pieces from 1920, and in major works: *Nacht* (Night) in 1927, and *Grünen Clowns* (Green Clowns), ◀ 47

tres pierres fines, que de diuers émaux, selon
le naturel desdites pensées : Le troisiesme
cerclè, remply de petites rozes de diamans
brillans, & de plusieurs perles rondes. Le
fōd couuert de petites enseignes de pierre-
ries & d'or, & la cime de plumaches de toute façon, & de longues & petites aigrettes,
au haut desquels il y en auoit vn d'excessiue
grosseur & haulteur. Les fraizes qu'ils por-
toient faites de fine dentelle fort grande, &
les manches plissées semblablement. Ils te-
noient chacun vn mouchoir de poinct coupé d'or & d'argent dans la main: les masques
dorez & découppez à piece emportée par
compartiment, tous lesquels ainsi parez fai-
soiēt vne entrée superbe, auec plusieurs en-
trelassemens, tant qu'ils se venoient ranger
en haye, six d'vn costé & six de l'autre. Alors
les viollons sonnoient la premiere partie de
leur Ballet. & lesdits Cheualliers changeant
de pas & de mesure, alloient former leur
premiere figure, laquelle suiuant l'Alphabet des anciēs Druides (trouué depuis quel-
ques années dans vn vieil monument) re-
presentoit vn caractere d'iceluy Alphabet
poinctè du nombre de douze, signifiant

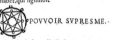 AMOVR PVISSANT.

35

De ceste premiere figure ils en formoiēt
vne seconde, representant aussi vn autre caractere dudit Alphabet, poinctè de mesme
nombre, lequel signifioit,

AMBITIEVX DESIR.

Et apres ceste seconde ils en faisoient
vne troisiesme d'vn autre caractere, signifiant

VERTVEVX DESSEIN.

Et puis ceste quatriesme qui signifioit,

RENOM IMMORTEL.

Les susdites figures se moquoient chacu-
ne d'vne cadance entiere, tournant ou re-
tournant en leur mesme place: puis apres
ces quatre, les viollons sonnoient la seconde partie du ballet, & les cheualliers d'vn
E iij.

---

autre pas plus gay & plus releué presque du
tout à capriolles, ils rentroient d'vn bel ordre en la cinquiesme figure, representant
aussi vn caractere, pointe du nombre susdit,
signifiant

GRANDEVR DE COV-
RAGE.

Et de la cinquiesme à ceste sixiesme, qui
signifioit

PEINE AGREABLE.

Puis la septiesme signifiant,

CONSTANCE ES-
PROVVEE.

Et la huitiesme signifioit

VERITE COGNEVE.

37

Apres ces huict figures bien formées &
bien distinctemēt representées. Les susdits
viollons sonnoient d'vn nouuel air la troisiesme & derniere partie dudit Ballet. Et les
douze Cheualliers changeans aussi d'vn
nouueau pas, venoient differemment à former la neufuiéme figure, representant vn
caractere dudit Alphabet, lequel signifioit

HEVREVX DESTIN.

Puis tomboient tousiours dançans en ceste dixiesme, dont le caractere signifioit

AIME DE TOVS.

En apres ils venoient marquer ceste vn-
ziesme, signifiant

COVRONNE DE
GLOIRE.

Et puis auec vne grauité superbe, ils for-
moient ceste derniere figure, marque du

---

plus parfaict caractere qui fust audit Alphabet, qui signifioit

POVVOIR SVPRESME.

A la fin de laquelle ils se trouuoient au
plus proche du theatre, où ils se reposoient
iusques à ce que le Roy commandoit, qu'ō
dançast des branles: & les violons commen-
çans à en sonner, lesdits Cheualiers alloiēt
chacun prendre pour dancer auec eux telle
Dame de la Cour qui leur plaisoit : & ayant
cōmencé la dāce, plusieurs autres seigneurs
& Gentils-hōmes qualifiez des plus dispots,
prenoiēt aussi d'autres Dames à leur fanta-
izie, & se mesloiēt auec lesdits Cheualiers &
seigneurs susdits audit bal, où toute sorte de
dance fust dancée en apres, tant en general
qu'en particulier, iusques à tant qu'il pleust
à sa Majesté de se retirer.

FIN.

with Bereska, in 1928. The cabaret's influence on Schoenberg appears most overtly in *Pierrot Lunaire* (1914).

Laban and Kandinsky in Munich. In 1899 Laban spent about three months in Munich studying with the sculptor/embroiderer Hermann Obrist, a somewhat underestimated yet outstanding teacher who espoused the Arts and Crafts Movement. Here Laban's childhood interest in several different media was given encouragement, and his youthful admiration for the skillfulness of the craftsman was confirmed. Obrist was also Kandinsky's informal teacher during the years 1899-1900, before Kandinsky enrolled formally in the Munich Academy studies under Franz Stuck. Obrist remained a firm friend of both men.

The important Munich period for Laban is 1910-1914, when he finally shifted his attention away from the graphic arts and began establishing himself as a dance theorist and practitioner. He spent 1910-12 in Munich, and thereafter passed his winters in Munich and his summers in Monte Verità, Ascona, until the declaration of war in late summer 1914.

◀ 48

Schwabing, Munich's famous artists' quarter, was Laban's neighborhood. He continued to earn his living as a graphic artist, publishing satirical drawings in the magazine *Jugend* and illustrating books. He studied early dance notation manuscripts, and the *Körperkultur* [2] methods of Mensendieck and Bode. He and his wife were avid theater and concert goers whenever they had the money. He also worked as an arranger of *Fasching* (Carnival) entertainments. This started in a small way in the winter of 1910-11 and increased until by 1913-14 he was already famed as a creator of inventive and sometimes satirical avant-garde productions for large numbers of carnival revellers.

Kandinsky's neighborhood from 1908 to 1914 was also Schwabing. He attended Wolfskehl's outrageous parties where similar activities to Laban's Fasching entertainments took place. Unlike Berlin, Munich's censorship allowed a relative freedom but the bohemian life style in Schwabing was often too much even for the Munich authorities, and lawsuits and arrests for excessive behavior in the streets were not uncommon.

Counterbalancing this lively physicality, both Laban and Kandinsky were interested in the teachings of Rudolf Steiner and of Madame Blavatsky. It is probable that Laban heard Steiner lecture in Paris in 1906, for he studied spiritual phenomena and religious practices while a student there. Kandinsky is known to have attended Steiner's lectures in Berlin in 1908. Steiner additionally lectured in Munich during this period. He had a particularly strong influence on Kandinsky, whose equilibrium was shaken by his views on the power of the spiritual world. However, both artists remained on the fringes of Steiner's Anthroposophy, and neither were members of Madame Blavatsky's Theosophical Society. Indeed Laban states in *Die Welt des Tänzers* (The Dancer's World) that Steiner "has got it wrong" in respect of the relation between movement and spirituality. Marie Steiner's *Eurythmy* exercises of breath, voice, and movement were to him an esoteric activity. Laban's vision was of a spiritual base to a much broader movement revolution, one that would touch the ordinary man, woman, and child.

1910-14 were momentous years for Kandinsky. He expressed his credo in *Über das Geistige in der Kunst* (Concerning the Spiritual in Art), a work of similar importance in his life to Laban's *Die Welt des Tänzers*. Although the Laban's key book not published until 1920, it was written early in World War I. Starting several years behind Kandinsky, Laban had to wait until 1914 to find his major growth points in dance theory. The years 1911-14 were a time of gestation and study, where movement and painting vied for his full attention. But the body in space was his true interest, and it inevitably led to dance.

Schoenberg's 12-tone composition technique and Laban's choreutic theory.
Schoenberg created a system of tonal play without a natural anchor, developing completely new rules in composition to replace those of the last three centuries. The tonal system is not a purely man-made compositional device. It is based on a formal and mathematical system of proportions of vibration, such that harmonic overtones sound through the chordal relations of octaves, fifths, fourths, thirds, and so on. In Schoenberg's twelve-tone system these intervals are eschewed. He provided self-imposed strategies for his tone rows, in which no one of the twelve chromatic tones

was more emphasized than another, as none was ever repeated until all twelve had been sounded. The natural laws of tonal music were replaced by an idiosyncratic choice of another set of constraints (the twelve-tone row) and manipulation techniques (retro, inverse, and retro-inverse), unfettered by conventional form, leading to a more spontaneous use of intellectually devised rules. His work was called "atonal," but he preferred the term "pluritonal."

Laban inherited the ballet tradition as his basic material. It is based on the octahedron, with the six directions of the vertical (up/down), the sagittal (front/back), and the lateral (right/left), which are embodied in steps (pas) and arm movements (ports de bras). These directions are passages through space, terminating in positions. They are grounded by the vertical line running through the dancer's spine and down to the point of support. This line, by which the dancer feels centered, is the grounded base to which the dancer returns and from which motion springs again. It is the ballet dancer's "doh." Laban saw further analogies between music and dance. For him, concurrent gestures of the limbs provide chords in space, harmonic tensions between the positions of the arms, legs, and head. Consecutive gestures create "trace forms" or melodic shapes in the "kinesphere," a term coined by Laban for the volume of space immediately surrounding each dancer. The kinesphere is analogous to the central registers of pitch in music, while the exaggerated registers are analogous in dance to the spatial areas very near the body's skin and very far from it, projected into the space beyond the body's reach. The six directions, and the *pas* and *ports de bras* derived from them, emphasize classical lines of balance and proportion which Laban found incompatible with his vision of a renaissance of the body and of dance as a contemporary art form capable of speaking the voice of disturbed and chaotic times.

Unlike Schoenberg, he did not devise an idiosyncratic method for his own compositional needs. Rather, he sought an expansion of the limited spatial base of classical ballet. He turned to the mundane movement forms of behavior, which had for some ten years been an object of study, and sought to find a spatial organizing principle in them, the so-called "choreological order." He found that behavior patterns rarely reflect the six directions of ballet, but consist in the more labile spatial forms of diagonals and diametrals, phrased in curves and angular forms. These, he found, could be idealized in an expanded model of twelve directions, the "icosahedron." Each of the classical six directions is opened out, doubled. Thus the vertical line at the center of ballet opens into a broad statement of up plus open and down plus open, giving four extensions of the limbs along lines running from the umbilicus to the shoulders and the hips. This stance, broad and assertive, contrasted with the fifth position of ballet, with its closed feet, narrow base, and soft, rounded, uplifted arms.

With his twelve-directional "scaffolding" for the kinesphere, Laban saw the possibility of a new theory of harmony applicable to dance, for which he coined the term "choreutics." Here he discovered, over several years of experimentation, an expansion of the port de bras exercises into sequences of movements which passed through the twelve directions, as spatial tone rows. These are termed "scales" and "rings," and consist of three, five, six, seven, or twelve parts. These scales, especially his "A" and "B" scales, were widely performed as basic training exercises for the body and became known as Laban's "swings," because of the way in which they were performed. All manner of variations were created on them, providing themes for studies and for dances.

Unlike Schoenberg's tone row, Laban's swings were harmonically based. Each scale is counterbalanced both in space and in the body, by inversion and transposition as harmonic opposites of perfect symmetry. These provide a balanced use of the body: opening plus forwards is matched by closing plus backwards, rising closed is matched by lowering open, turning to the right by turning to the left, flying jumps by sprawling falls.

Laban did not abandon the six directions. He included them as stable contrasts to his new labile and off-balance scales, thus providing a further harmonically contrasted experience for his dancers.

The fundamental link between Laban and Schoenberg lies in their innovative treatment of the harmonic system of their medium. They share the need for change, but

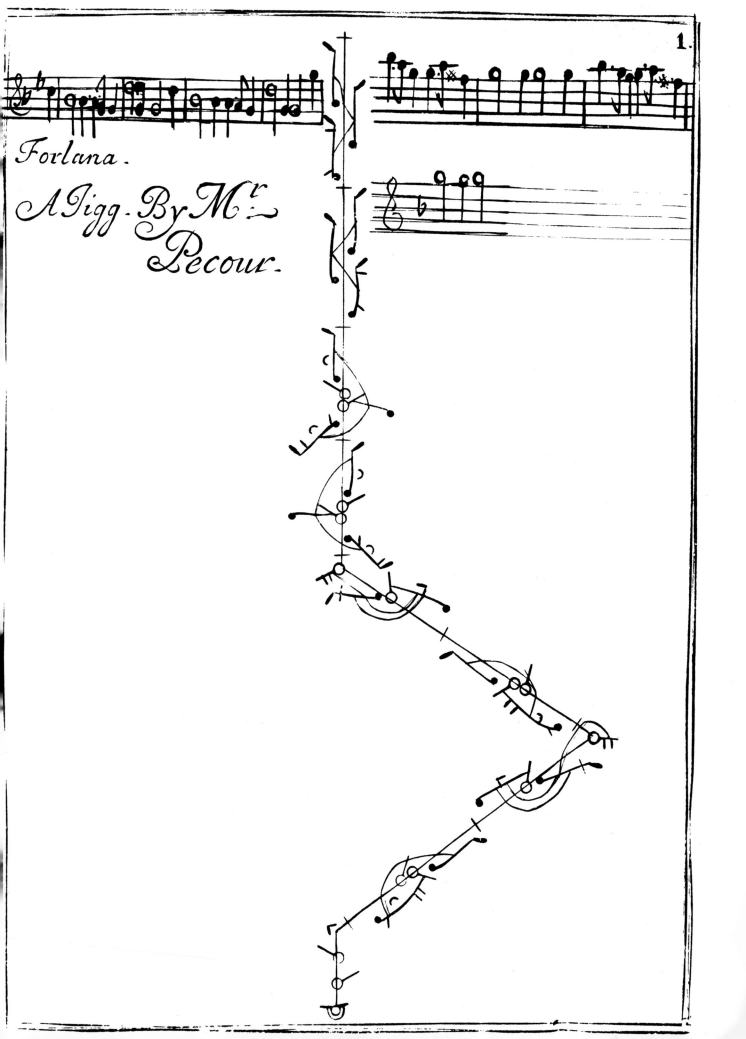

Forlana.

A Jigg. By Mr.
Pecour.

their motivation is starkly contrasted. Schoenberg sought a break with previous tradition and a new system for his personal use. Laban sought an expansion of the existing tradition in harmony with the human body, to be used by everybody, an expansion which would reflect the freer philosophy of the twentieth century.

Kandinsky's form and color theory; Laban's eukinetics. Kandinsky expressed line as "the imprint of energy — the visible trace of the invisible." Laban described the dancer's gestures in space as "trace forms" in "the land of silence." The "invisible" and the "land of silence" were the very real spiritual world. The dancer had to enter it, and to let its changing forms and rhythms be embedded in his movement. For Laban it was a world of terrifying powers, for Kandinsky it was the source of the inner need which must express itself in form and color. The organic element in art and the mimetic gesture in dance were "falling away," and abstract patterns were taking over as meaningful in their own right. Made up of innumerable combinations of form and color in painting, and of form and rhythm in dance movement, they reflected the harmonic resonances of the soul, in relationships that were both balanced and grotesque.

50 ▶

Kandinsky described his theory of color harmony as six related vibrations, of blue, green, yellow, orange, red, and violet, divided into two groups of warm and cold colors. Laban's dynamic qualities in the dancer's movement were the six qualities of lightening or strengthening in force, quickening or sustaining in time, focusing or diffusing in space. These were divided into two groups of "fighting against" and "indulging in" the elements of forcefulness, temporality, and spatiality. Thus a lightening/sustaining/diffusing quality contrasted with a strengthening/quickening/focusing one. For Kandinsky, black and white were additionally separated out as two kinds of silences: white, which is pregnant with possibilities, and black, which is as dead, as nothingness. Laban's additional factor was flow, in which the movement quality shifted between unfettered fluidity and binding stillness.

For Kandinsky, every artist had to express what was peculiar to him, his own vision of harmony and disharmony. Likewise for Laban, each dancer had to express

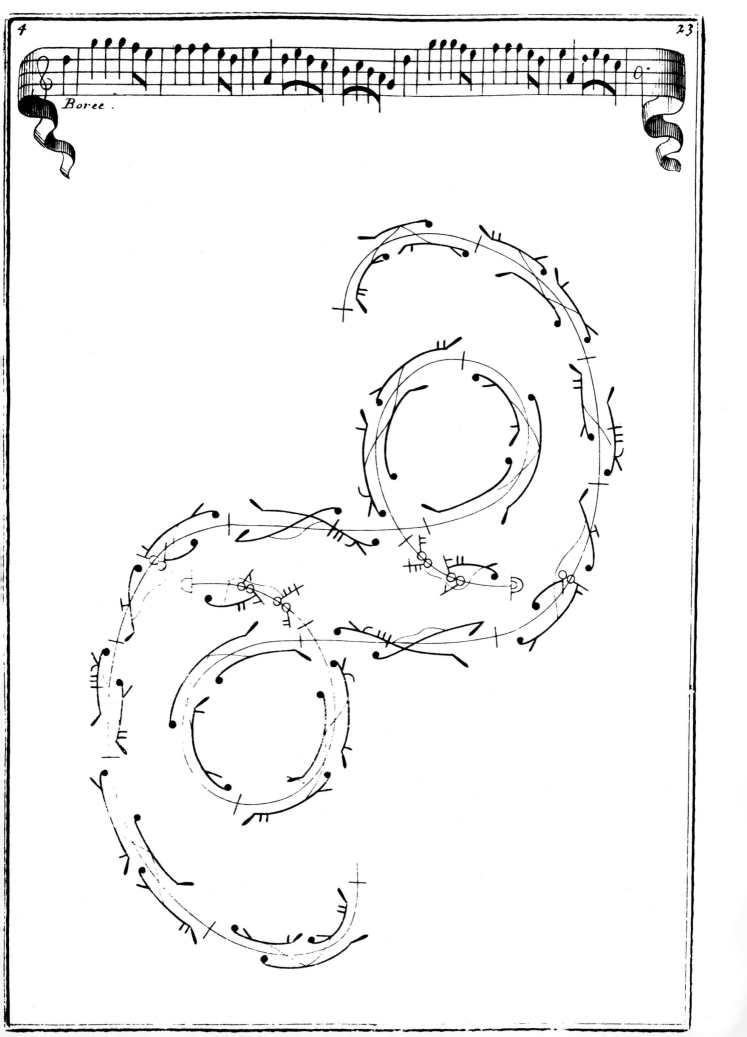

Boree.

his own inner voice. But for dancers there was the additional form of dancing together, a world of celebration, communion and community. One of Laban's first actions after he decided to devote his time to dance instead of graphic art was to mount a poster campaign in Munich for a revolution in social dance as a new form of communal artistic movement.

Kandinsky was also interested in dance. "Ballet at present is in a state of chaos," he wrote. "The new dancing is being evolved as... the only means of giving the real inner meaning in terms of time and space." He had seen Isadora Duncan's attempts and Fokine's choreography at Diaghilev's *Ballets Russes*, and had himself worked with the Russian dancer Alexander Sacharoff in experiments on the movement interpretation of color. At the time Kandinsky was writing (1911), Laban had not yet started his work, but it was he who would fulfill Kandinsky's prophecy for the establishment of the abstract in dance.

The Gesamtkunstwerk. At the same time as they completely revolutionized their compositional techniques, all three men asked another question. Art forms are separate, different, distinct; but do they have to be isolated? What happens when they co-exist in a work, not as a potpourri of mixed-up media but as independent, equally valid, co-existing partners?

Kandinsky envisaged the emergence of a new stage art in which "musical movement, pictorial movement, and physical movement combine... interwoven in harmony and discord." His *Die Gelbe Klang* (Yellow Sound) was his first developed work of this sort, after tentative beginnings with *Riesen* (Giants), *Der grüne Klang* (Green Sound), and *Schwarz und Weiss* (Black and White). Initially conceived in 1909, *Die Gelbe Klang* was nearly ready for production in 1914, with Thomas von Hartmann's music half-written; but World War I prevented its performance. Without plot, the motion of marionette-like people, giants, light, and sound all interplay in a manner unlike anything seen before. This originality was not total art as Wagner understood it, but a new genre allowing the arts to play independent, co-existing roles, which the audience could appreciate as interactions. Throughout his life, Kandinsky retained an intense desire to create large stage works, but he was never able to fully realize them.

Schoenberg's *Die Glückliche Hand* (The Lucky Hand) was also ready in 1914, and was actually performed in 1924. It had a plot, a text, and the characters of Man, Woman, Gentlemen, and Workers, with one singing role and the rest mute. Lighting changes, costume color, props, and a musical score complete the content of the Drama with Music (Opus 18).

Laban's school in Munich was a "Schule für Tanz-Ton-Wort und Plastik" (School for Dance, Sound, Word and Plastic Arts), and his best-known multi-media work was his *Sang an die Sonne* (Song to the Sun) in 1917 on Monte Verità. The work took nature itself as the set, the lighting being the setting sun at dusk, bonfires at midnight, and the rising sun at dawn. The audience had to traipse up the mountain three times! The movement of groups of dancers was improvised and they made the sound themselves, vocally and by playing percussion instruments. It was more a ritual than a stage work, and took place as part of the celebrations of the "Orientalische Templar Ordnung," a freemasonry group.

In *Pierrot Lunaire* (1914) Schoenberg experimented with "Sprechgesang," the use of a half-singing, half-speaking voice. Laban also undertook voice experiments as study techniques in his schools in Munich and Zurich. In 1922 in Hamburg, he experimented with speech choir accompaniment in his large work *Faust Erlösung* (Faust's Redemption), and later in *Grünen Clowns* (Green Clowns, 1928) with body and voice sounds, sneezes, coughs, and body sounds made by the dancers as they moved.

Wartime. The war saw the three men divided. They never returned to as close an affinity again, but the web of artistic interrelations continues. Kandinsky returned to Russia immediately after war was declared, and continued a career in painting and teaching, visiting Sweden and Finland. After the Revolution he was active as an administrator of art museums and art teaching. He returned to Germany in 1922 to take up a professorship at the Bauhaus in Weimar. Schoenberg was in Berlin at the outbreak of hostilities, lecturing at the Stern Conservatory. He had to return to Vienna to report for military service in 1915; he was discharged two years later on medical

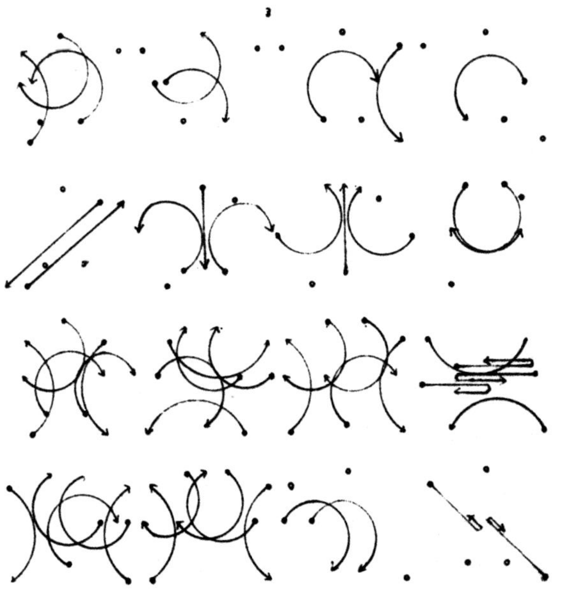

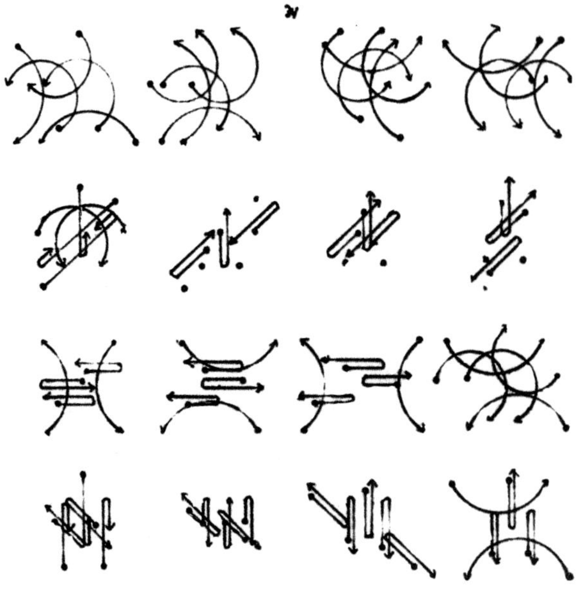

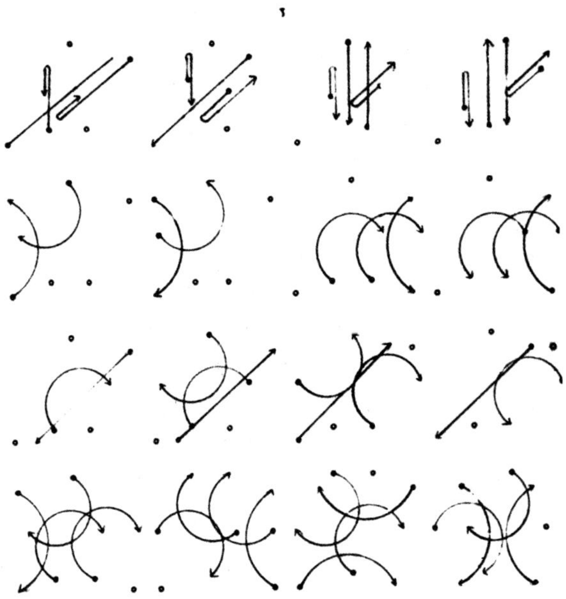

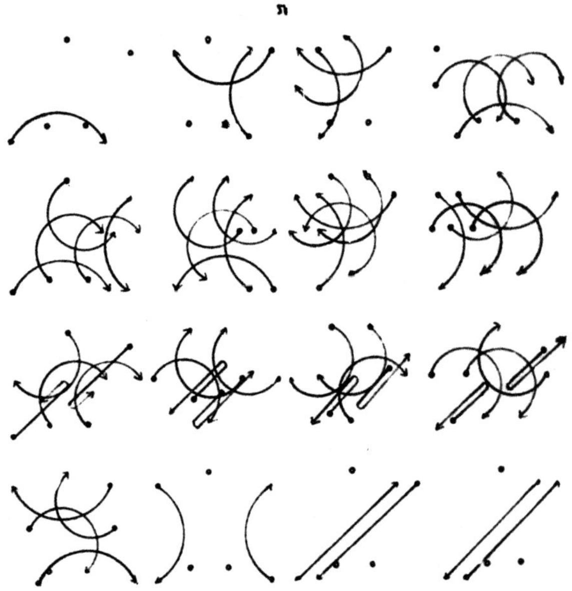

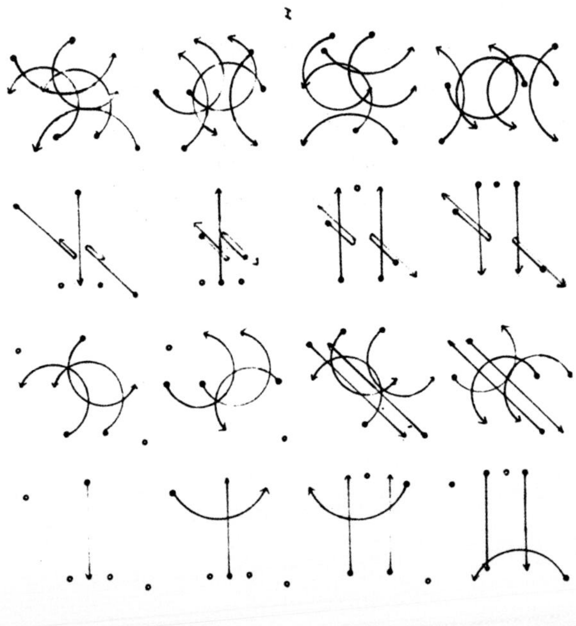

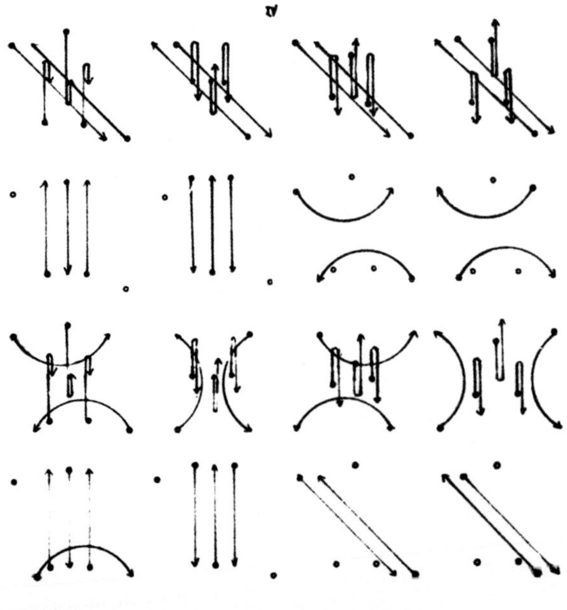

grounds. His musical output was interrupted during this time, but he continued to wrestle with the structural problems of his move away from tonality.

Laban was at his Summer School at Monte Verità in Switzerland when war was declared. He moved to Zurich in spring 1915 and reopened his School there. He was penniless and ill throughout this period, living on a knife edge. His dilemma was that to be allowed to remain in Switzerland by the Swiss authorities, he had to be solvent and be well enough to work; but good health left him vulnerable to the Austrians' demand that he do military service. Nevertheless he managed to further his ideas by intense research with his pupil Marie Wiegmann and his friend Suzanne Perrottet[3], with his wife Maja Lederer running the schools. Only one work, *Der Spielmann* (The Fiddler) was created during this period, apart from the extraordinary Sang an die Sonne at Ascona in 1917.

Prestigious positions and shifts of philosophy. Kandinsky was employed at the Bauhaus under Gropius in 1922, and entered a period in which logic seemed to replace some of the spiritual criteria for his work. He referred to an emerging "science of art," and to the merger of the plastic arts with science and industry, as in the Bauhaus rationale. In his continuing experiments with synthesis of the arts, the dance was now so abstract that it became the motion of pure spatial forms in a theater setting. At the Bauhaus his colleague Oskar Schlemmer produced dances of a highly abstract style in which the figures were masked by geometrical costumes. Although it was Mary Wigman's pupil Gret Palucca who was most directly in touch with Kandinsky, Laban too was familiar with Oskar Schlemmer. They were working quite differently in purpose and form, and agreed to co-exist without comment.

◄51

In 1926 Kandinsky published *Punkt und Linie zu Fläche* (Point and Line to Plane), an analysis of "pictorial elements" in the Bauhaus series of publications. In 1928, Laban completed the work on his twenty-year search for a notation of movement and published his *Kinetography* (now known as Labanotation); at the same conference he launched a "science of dance" called Choreology (now Choreological Studies). Both men complemented their visionary pre-World War I period with these much more objective contributions to the study of their art. What they had realized only through spiritual conviction - a totally new approach to color, form, rhythm, and harmony - was now underpinned by a new theory and, in Laban's case, by the possibility of dance literacy.

For Laban this was only a shift of emphasis. He called himself an artist/researcher, and he continued to work with both a spiritual vision and an analytic curiosity throughout his life. 1928 was simply a culminating year for his work towards dance literacy and a structural knowledge of dance. He moved on, as he always did, to search in areas such as the dynamics of movement and the relationship of the psychological and physical in movement, work which he did not publish until the 1940s and 1950s. His artistic output at this time was still spiritually based, but his career as a performer had ended by 1928 because of an accident on stage.

52 ▶

Both men were concerned with broadening the base of the pedagogy of their art. Kandinsky felt that specialist training without a general human basis was no longer possible (as he stated in his 1928 publications, "Art Pedagogy" and "Analytical Drawings"). Laban's *Gymnastik und Tanz* (Exercise and Dance, 1926), and later Modern Educational Dance (1948) promoted the rudiments of a "free dance technique" in which his concepts of form in the body (choreutics) and rhythm in the body (eukinetics) were fully conceived. Unlike Kandinsky, Laban's "dance for all" policy promoted celebratory community dance. He envisaged and created a new form of art experience for amateurs — the choric dance. City movement choirs, like speech choirs and singing choirs, were founded. His works *Lichtwende* (Dawning Light), *Fausts Erlösung* (Faust's Redemption), and Titan were danced by vast numbers of men and women, usually in an outside location.

It was during this period (1922-1928) that Laban's major theater dance works were staged by his large company "Tanzbühne Laban" and his small company "Kammertanzbühne Laban." They followed each other with incredible rapidity. He was self-employed, in permanent financial trouble, but always able to surmount his difficulties. He opened some twenty-five schools across Germany, and more in neighboring countries. He became the undoubted leader of New German Dance, with Mary Wigman as its outstanding performing artist.

Merce Cunningham

Schoenberg and Laban both moved to Berlin. In 1925 Schoenberg was glad to accept a teaching position in the Prussian Academy of Fine Arts. In this prestigious post, he enjoyed a reasonably affluent and much respected position as an outstanding composition teacher for six years. His own composing continued with the beginnings of public recognition. Although he never set out to create a system of composition to be used by others, his twelve-tone system became one of the most widely influential musical methods of the century. In 1930 Laban was appointed to the two most prestigious jobs in dance: choreographer at the Bayreuth Wagner Festival, in 1930 and 1931; director of movement at the Berlin State Theaters including the Unter den Linden Opera House, where he was given a four-year contract.

Their writings. For all three men, writing about their visions and their theories was a part of their artistic life. Laban's writings are difficult to read, because he is verbally undisciplined. His first language was Hungarian, with German and French as second and third languages; but he was not a gifted linguist. He had the enormous challenge of trying to coin new words and phrases to express his concepts about human movement. While this problem was shared by all three men, for Laban it was doubly difficult. There was no tradition of scholarly writing in dance on which he could build. Language is notoriously dualist, while he was trying to express a unitary approach to movement as a simultaneous physical, mental, and spiritual act. Strict oppositions like inner/outer, or body/mind, were inadequate. Terms like "attitude" referred to either body attitude, as in a posture, or mental attitude, but not both. Thus Laban's writings tend to fumble for terminology to express what can only be experienced through kinaesthetic perception. He had inadequate means of illustrating his texts, while Kandinsky's publications were full of examples of paintings, and Schoenberg's with tone rows in music notation. This was Laban's weak point, for he knew that dance literacy was essential for communication. His descriptions read either prosaically when he attempted an external view of movement, or rapturously when he attempted phenomenological description of the event from within.

Nevertheless, *Die Welt des Tänzers* (1920) established his reputation as a leading figure in innovative dance and as the first dance writer to address central issues.

Gymnastik und Tanz (Exercise and Dance, 1926), and *Des Kindes Gymnastik und Tanz* (Exercise and Dance for Children, 1926) were essential text books for the teachers of his many schools, encapsulating his educational philosophy and practice, while *Choreographie* (1926) was his first attempt to express his growing understanding of logical order in dance and ways of notating dance. Its interest extends beyond its content, for Laban was so irrepressibly creative that while writing the book he moved on both conceptually and in the symbol system he was using. The reader has to follow his leaps of thought. The 1928 publication of his notation under the name *Tanzschrift* (dance writing) confirmed him as the intellectual and practical leader of German Modern Dance. *Schrifttanz* (1928-31), a journal published by Universal-Edition to promote his notation, established him further, especially as he widened its scope to include discussion of essential issues on dance philosophy, status, education, and practice. His articles, published in arts and theater magazines as well as ethical, satirical and political journals, were copious. In 1935 he wrote an autobiography, *Ein Leben für den Tanz* (A Life for Dance), in which he portrayed himself as a spiritually based artist, social critic and visionary practitioner.

In England he wrote five influential books: *Effort* (1947), after his wartime work in industrial motion study; *Modern Educational Dance* (1948), an outline for teachers of the newly-established creative dance in primary and secondary schools; *Mastery of Movement on the Stage* (1950), on his methods for actors, mime artists, and dramatic dancers; and *Principles of Dance and Movement Notation* (1956). *Choreutics* (published posthumously in 1966) sets out his concepts of analysis of space and dynamics in the body. His outstanding spatial imagination for the dance makes difficult reading, but the book contains a level of insight not attempted before in the domain of dance. Sadly, his writings inadequately express his art, which could only be communicated practically. Laban's dances and dance practices live only in the memory of his students, since his notation, like film recording, came too late for his major choreographies. It is not surprising that adequate study of his early work is so elusive.

Departure under the Third Reich*.* The rise of the National Socialist Party was traumatic for all three men. It was first felt in the unnecessary and unintentional

TRIO ÉPOUVANTABLE.

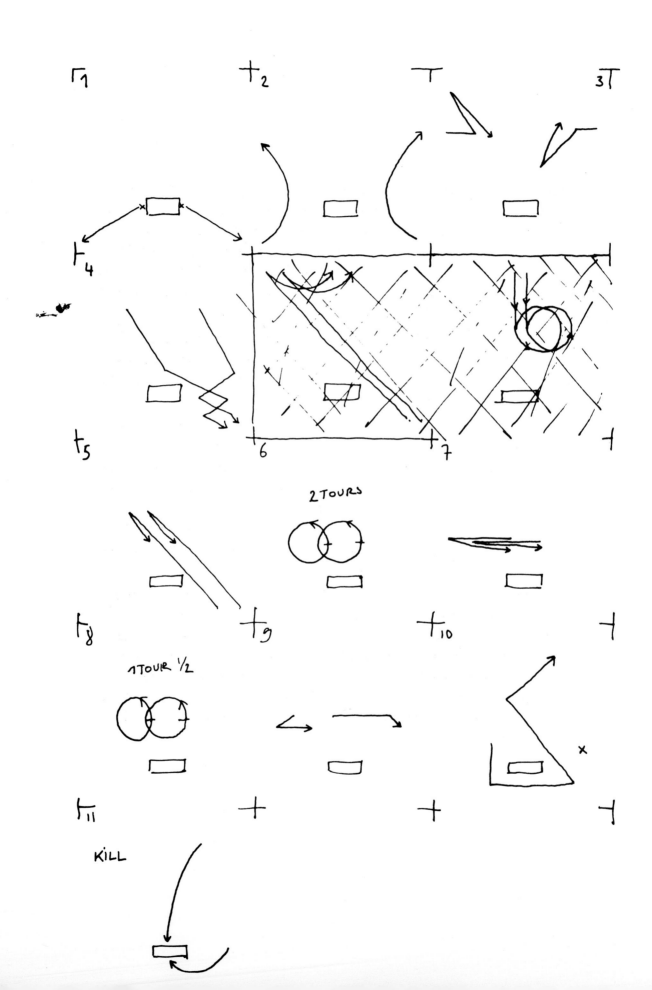

breakdown of friendship between Kandinsky and Schoenberg, after Kandinsky made a reference to the "Jewish Problem" in his correspondence in 1923. Always conscious of anti-Semitism and personally harassed since 1920, Schoenberg was deeply wounded and never communicated with Kandinsky again. In 1932 he was dismissed from his post, along with all the Jews at the Prussian Academy. He emigrated to the U.S.A. forthwith, where he settled in Los Angeles and began a new career as a renowned teacher, composer, and writer.

In 1933 the Bauhaus was forcibly closed down. Kandinsky emigrated to France, to settle in Neuilly-sur-Seine. The Nazis confiscated his known works and he featured prominently in their exhibition of "Degenerate Art" in Munich in 1937. With his wife Nina, he continued a quiet life as a painter and writer.

Laban, a political innocent, stayed on, becoming employed by the Ministry of Propaganda to promote German dance throughout Germany and abroad. But he fell foul of the Nazis in 1936 with his work *Vom Tauwind und der neuen Freude* (Thawing Wind and the New Happiness), a choreography for massed amateurs at the dance festival of the Berlin Olympic Games. Like Kandinsky, his works were banned and derided. His books were burned. After a period of house arrest he managed to reach Paris late in 1937, where Kurt Jooss, his pupil, rescued him and brought him in a state of destitution to Dartington Hall in England.

◄ 53

The tragedy for Laban was that he could not emigrate and continue making art. Dancers need people, places, schools, and companies, all of which are built up over many years of training. Laban never choreographed again. By 1942 he had started a new career as movement adviser to wartime industry in Manchester, and his work on creative dance spread into schools for disturbed patients. His principles of movement and dance and his system of notation revolutionized dance study throughout the English-speaking world, through his German pupils who emigrated to the U.S.A., Australia, South Africa, and Britain.

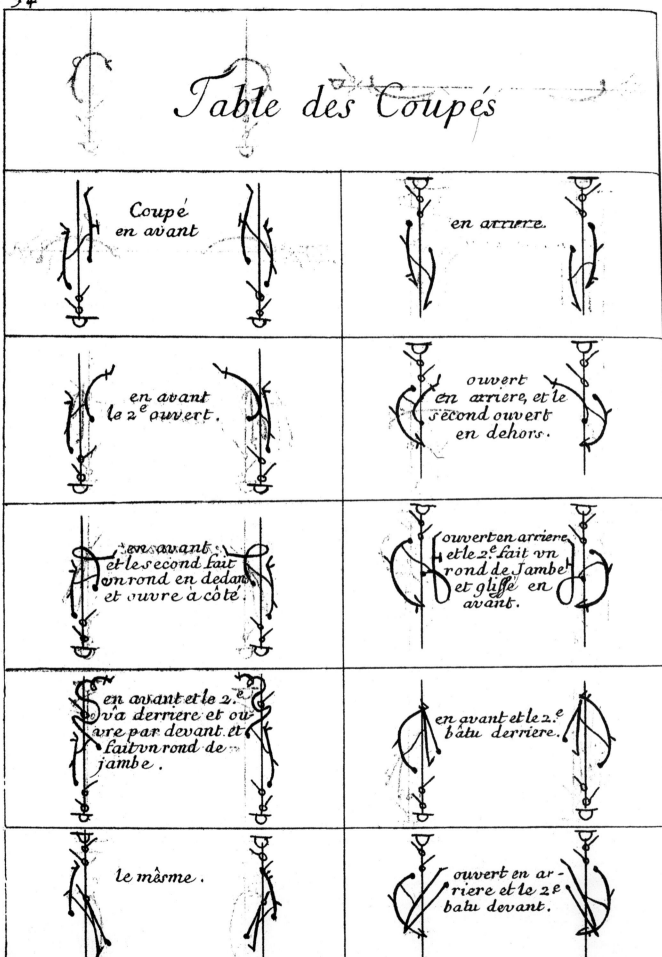

Table des Coupés

Coupé en avant

en arriere.

en avant le 2.e ouvert.

ouvert en arriere, et le second ouvert en dehors.

en avant et le second fait un rond en dedans et ouvre à côté.

ouvert en arriere et le 2.e fait un rond de Jambe et glissé en avant.

en avant et le 2.e va derriere et ouvre par devant et fait un rond de jambe.

en avant et le 2.e batu derriere.

le mêsme.

ouvert en arriere et le 2.e batu devant.

NOTATIONS AND DRAWINGS

This study is confined to notations which relate to dance or, at least, to the artistic intention of movement in general. The aim here is not to go through Anne Hutchinson-Guest's exhaustive list of eighty-one systems for notating movement, including sixty-two for the modern age alone, which for our purposes dates from the work of Stepanov in 1892 (the first project to lay claim to universality). Systems involving bio-mechanics alone, or kinesics, like the well-known notation of Birdwhistell in the United States, have been deliberately left out of this study. Moreover, it also becomes apparent that systems whose prime objectives include dance, and the imaginational world of the body, have proved to be an infinitely wealthy source of material. These systems have brought to life previously undreamt-of facets of the human body, facets which have been put to good use in numerous fields of knowledge, including anthropology, etiology, therapeutics, ergonomics, etc...

Among the systems related to the history of dance, we have singled out those which have effectively characterized a stage, a rupture or a renewal in the thinking on movement and the representation of movement, even when this system was little, or even entirely unknown. However, in our determination to maintain clarity, including clarity of information, we adhere to certain systems of classification established by Hutchinson-Guest. These include, among others, the division of types of notation according to the concrete elements of their codification (which do not neceassarily predetermine the way they function). In other words, notation is either represented in verbal form, written in letters, mathematical symbols, in abstract codification, pictograms or figurines (stick-figures), or it is represented musically, traced, or in the form of a ground plan.

Finally, we contribute our personal point of view and evaluation, giving criteria of judgement and sensibility which together serve to place our approach in a context which is not only artistic, but also aesthetic and historical.

Manuscript of the Basses Danses from Cervera and Tarragona, Spain 1495

This document, which was discovered thirty years ago by local folklorists, constitutes the first attempt at abstract symbolization of danced figures. Remarkable progress towards an interpretation of this document has been achieved by the dancer Carles Mas Garcia, who claims that this manuscript presents an entirely original compromise between verbal abbreviation and spatial representation. As this document needs to be read vertically, it induces a linear reading of movement. ◀ 54

The Cervera system, an alphabet of five signs each referring to the figures involved in low-dance (the scholarly dance at that time, made up of merely five figures), functions as a series of ideograms based on complex unities.

It is rather surprising that this document existed at a time when, throughout the whole of Europe, verbal description or initials, were used as the prime means of archiving dance figures. It is even possible that the existence of popular scores of *contrapas* dances in the nineteenth century bears witness, as Mas Garcia suggests even today, to a "Catalan" tendency in the activity of dance notation. (cf. C. Mas Garcia, *Approximaciao a la tecnica coregrafica del contrapas*, Barcelona, 1983).

Thoinot Arbeau, *L'Orchésographie*, Langres, France, 1588

This work represents an important stage in notation due to its break with linearity, such that the danced text no longer follows the line of verbal writing, nor the sequence of musical notes, from left to right. Instead, the text was arranged in tablatures like those used by lutenists and guitarists, which gave rise to a new spatial organization of the signs. Moreover, since the range of vocabulary had become considerably more extensive, abbreviations were replaced by the name of the figure. Texts and pictograms served to complete the instructions.

Caroso, *Nobilità di Dame*, Italy, 1610

Caroso presents the first examples of baroque "ground plans" such as they existed during the same year in *Le ballet de Mgr le Duc de Vendôme* in France. These involved planimetrical figures with an esoteric dimension, which spectators read by looking down from above. The idea of dance as the "arcanum" of an arch-writing of the world was already to be found in *Le ballet comique de la Reine* in 1581. This prefigured the famous "alphabet of the druids," for it must not be forgotten that, among druids, writing was forbidden by religious injunction.

John Playford, *The English Dancing Master, England*, 1650

Parallel to his short descriptions of figures, Playford uses a ground plan in the form of a rose window to indicate the arrangement of dancers at the start of a quadrille, this dance here being intended for gatherings at English manor houses. His innovation entails a different sign each time, one to indicate the man, one the woman.

André Lorin, *Le livre de la contredanse du Roi,* France, 1688

The work of Lorin deserves our attention both on the merit of his plastic innovations, and of the set of symbolic components he brings together in order to define the purpose of the quadrille, these being given in the form of diagrams, pictograms and even colored symbols. Although Lorin's work was disregarded by Louis XIV and the Royal Academy of Dance, it comprises elements of analysis which were clearly taken up in the work of Feuillet later on.

Raoul-Auger Feuillet, *Chorégraphie*.1700

It is most likely that the invention of this system can be attributed to Pierre Beauchamps, who was called upon, following a decree passed by parliament in 1671, to find a system for the fixation and transmission of dance. A document, written in his own handwriting, which dates from well before 1700, provides evidence of Feuillet's indebtedness to Beauchamps. Like Arbeau, Beauchamps and Feuillet strove to discover the primary element (the step) which could act as a grammatical common denominator, one which dance could utilize and develop in an increasingly complex manner. The idea of focusing this common denominator on the foundation of the very source of all movement (the transfer of weight) is still a source of curiosity for dancers today, as a result of its reliance on the force of intuition. In graphic terms, this consists in a base line drawn along an axis, which traces the course and development of laterality around the axis of the body. This type of writing was used continually until the end of the baroque period, during which time it was subjected to highly admirable graphic variations throughout the whole of Europe. This system embodied, therefore, the first attempt at conceiving of dance and movement in global terms, employing genuinely aesthetic ideas and a precise lexical corpus.

De la Cuisse, *le Répertoire du bal*, 1752

Besides a number of scores from the same period, these notations testify to an extreme impoverishment of dance (in the rustic style of the quadrille) and its writing. This work contains simple floor plans, showing the iconical transposition of foot movement ("step") as can be found in the whole repertoire of popular dances, as late as the "foxtrot" by Warhol...

Théleur, *Letters on Dancing*, G.B., 1831

Taylor, the dancing master who, having established his reputation, francisized his name to Théleur, set out to apply some ideas of Blasis and thus identify seven basic elements of movement which could be structured around the musical range of a "ballet" score. This research triggered off the first stages of the romantic subordination of movement to a musical composition, in contrast to the baroque period, in which movement was articulated according to a modular musical structure. This system finds echoes in the work of Stepanov.

Saint Léon, *la Sténochorégraphie*, France, 1852

Arthur de Saint Léon, a highly talented choreographer and dancer, perfected a purely pictographic system which takes into account the structural aspects of figures in classical ballet. He employs stylized figurines, articulated along the lines of musical structures.

Léon presents the image of dance in strictly visual terms, and discards all elements pertaining to physical functions.

Zorn, *Grammatik der Tanzkunst*, Germany, 1887

Friedrich Albert Zorn was a respectable master of ballet, whose authority in matters of academic orthodoxy was acknowledged as far abroad as the United States. His "grammar of dance" was intended to give details indicating correct positioning, as well as correct enchaînement. Zorn's little pictograms go beyond the purely formal outlook of Saint Léon by likening the figures of dancers to characters from abstract comic strips. This may appear thoroughly amusing from today's perspective, especially as each movement is demonstrated in a separate vignette, each representing only the section of body concerned by the particular movement.

Vladimir Ivanovich Stepanov, *Alphabet des mouvements du corps humain*, France, 1892

This work marked a fundamental turning point in the history of dance notation, instigated by a dancer who originally came from Russia, and subsequently studied anatomy and orthopaedics in France. For the first time ever, movement is here approached from a universal point of view, without relying on the authority of the preexistent vocabulary of an established school or a specific choreographic trend.

Even if this system forms part of the long series of systems written according to musical patterns, Stepanov uses it not as a structural framework, but as the basis of a diagram, which incorporates music with the help of a note, similar to a musical note, but one which represents a driving force in dance, rather than a tonal value. "Keys," like those of Benesh in the twentieth century, later served to modify and influence the character of the elements. The scope covered by Stepanov can be divided into several linear unities, in which the lines refer to the articulations of the levers in question.

The Stepanov system is abstract, and largely functional, dealing with flexion, torsion and extension. It was integrated into the program of teaching at the Imperial School of Dance, the first institution to adopt such teaching methods since the baroque period. Although Stepanov's system aimed to apply a universal approach to dance, it was soon applied more specifically to the canons of classical ballet. It must be underlined, however, that Stepanov always captured the keen interest of his followers, for his work continued to win fervent appreciation from the greatest dancers of Russian ballet.

Nijinski adapted the Stepanov system to his needs, before going on to create more spatialized models of his own. In her articles and conferences, Ann Hutchinson-Guest points out the "blank spots" which Nijinski identifies in the system.

The question as to whether Stepanov's system represents either a blatent paradox, or the rejection of the systematic continuity of writing, is a source of fascination, and marks the beginning of modernity in dance.

Alfred Giraudet, *Mimique, Physionomie et Gestes*, France, 1892

This disciple of Delsarte had the strange idea of encoding, quantifying and classifying expressions, especially those of the face. Giraudet here takes over from where Delsarte left off, on the subject of the general deciphering of the semic elements of the human body. The aim of this work is equally scientific and artistic in character, and prefigures the research of the American kinesic school, as well as the studies in non-verbal communication which followed in its wake.

Margaret Morris, *The Notation of Movement*, England, 1920

Morris was the first woman writer of notation, and the first to be deeply involved in modern dance. As a friend of the Duncans, she was influenced by their work on the development and movement of figures painted on the side of Greek vases, as well as the approach of Maurice Emmanuel to this subject. Her notation, whose aims were therapeutic, pedagogical and artistic in nature, emphasizes the importance of the axis as the place where movement originates. This system of notation is still taught in some institutions in Britain.

Rudolf von Laban (Rudolf Laban), *Schrifttanz*, Germany, 1928

Laban is to theory and dance notation what Freud is to psychoanalysis, both father and revolutionary, legislator and opponent. His notation brought about a considerable upheaval of concepts related to movement, and his thinking deserves to be recognized as one of the most innovative of its kind developed during the twentieth century.

Laban's notation cannot be accounted for outside the wider context of his choreological thinking. This notation is based on the primacy of two purely sensory elements, that of "weight," and that of the quality of the energy, or "flux," governing its movement. In order to notate, and give meaning to these previously imperceptible elements, Laban refers back to Feuillet's system, which involves dividing the body into two lateral parts along the propagation axis. The signs he uses draw qualitative comparisons between data concerning weight and energy, and visible driving structures, where the latter only occur as a consequence and as a form of expression of the dynamics. Notation concerning intensity is indicated with symbols of varying colors (ranging from white to black), while notation concerning time is distinguished by the actual size of the graphic markings.

One of the innovative features of Laban's notation was its break with linearity (from left to right) as employed by the majority of systems, and its tendency to project the body along the sky-earth axis instead, which corresponds more closely to the body's natural axis. It is worth noting, however, that Laban himself was not destined to bring his project to its successful conclusion, and master the system as a whole. A good portion of the merit for this must be attributed to his faithful and excellent disciple, Albrecht Knust, who perfected Laban's initial directions.

The fact that the Laban school continues to pursue research which has always remained open, both as far as philosophical and practical precepts are concerned, only serves to prove the tremendous interest shown in this work. Laban's notation is not merely a system, but an entire school of thought.

Pierre Conté, *Traité d'Ecriture de la Danse*, France, 1931

Pierre Conté was a many-faceted personality, one who inspired fascination as a result of his lively intuition and wide-ranging field of research. However, he also disconcerted his public as a result of his preference for isolation, and his lack of interest in modernity in dance (although it must be said that his notation does nevertheless contain certain modern elements). In turn, Conté was drawn to a variety of activities as diverse as military life, Marey's biomechanics, music, and traditional forms of music and dance. It can be assumed that, having studied time-lapse photography, Conté must have born in mind the fact that the most important factor emerging from movement is that of dynamics. In spite of the remarkable dedication of Michèle Nadal[1], who endeavored to continue this teaching in France, Conté's notation has never given rise to a bustling circle of thought, analysis, and creation of the sort which sprouted around Laban's notation in the United States. Unlike Laban, "Conté notation" has regrettably remained bound by its national limits, even though it has proved to be a valuable source of interest as regards sensibility in dance.

Although Conté notation conforms to the system of musical notation, its musicality is not confined to the realm of symbolization. It also draws inspiration from material which is common to both music and dance, like *tempo*

(Laban reminded us that the nature of choreographic tempo was distinct from musical tempo, and claimed, like M. Wigman, that movement produces its own duration), but also, and more particularly, from material like accents and nuances. Thanks to the factors he derives from the field of music, Conté was able to organize the nature of movement into a systematic network of "intensity" and "placing."

The author himself very quickly directed Conté notation towards the task of deciphering and "translating" documents relating to traditional and ancient dance. Francine Lancelot had recourse to this type of notation when first approaching her study of scores dating from the period of Beauchamps-Feuillet.

Alwin Nikolais, *The Choroscript*, 1944

Nikolais' system of notation was composed in the makeshift huts of the Allied armies in England during the Normandy invasion. This system has its origins in the teaching of Wigman and Holm, and logically bears

the traces of the influence of Laban; it maintains Laban's idea that mainspring events in dance can be said to spread out from a central axis. However, instead of basing his study on the point of support of the foot, and on the centrifugal maintenance of blocks of "weight" as unities of meaning, Nikolais takes a critical stance at Laban's neglect of rhythm and applies his knowledge of music in order to establish a representation of a much more musically inspired notion of movement. Such a notion of movement is, moreover, intended to unfold in a much more tightly knit fashion, from one pole of the body to the other, according to its own artistic principles of spiraling, where movement spreads out from the center to the periphery.

It is regrettable that this fine system, whose graphic qualities can readily be explained on the basis of the pictorial and plastic nature of its author's own leanings, has never been the subject of a publication. At the very most, Nikolais used this system as a pedagogical tool in his lessons. The prolific range of

1. Plan large se resserre
sur affiche.
p.image d'un groupe et la
démarche bizarre, puis de l'hyper epai.

qnd le radio s'est soudain
quitté d'otto qui s'arrête
de dos.

2. paroles incompréhensibles de
la caissière

3. main farfouillent boutons, gestes
réglés 4. sortie d'un ticket.

5. traveling sur les 3 chauds qui
trébuchent. replient leurs têtes
rentrent dans la garde →

qui rentre dans otto ↓
qui dégringole dans les
lamions molles ↙

activities of this creator has, up till now, prevented him from devoting time to making this notation better known to a wider public, even though he considers it to be of universal interest. There is a pressing need, therefore, to see the publication of a fully annotated version of the *Choroscript*.

Rudolf Benesh, *An Introduction to Benesh Dance Notation*, G.B., 1956

This painter, a newcomer to the world of dance who disregarded the whole tradition of notation, sought to establish a system capable of providing dancers with a written score. He launched into this research after being spurred by the sight of his wife, Joan, struggling to memorize movements for her performances with the Saddler's Welles Ballet Company. Benesh also has recourse to the scalar device operating in music, in which each stave corresponds to a section of the body. The symbolic unity refers to a driving event, classed according to its anatomical distribution (at joints, or extremities, etc.), and can be modi-

fied by a series of extremely subtle "keys" which are, among other things, often used to organize the third dimension very efficiently.

Elegant and well laid out on the page, Benesh notation gives priority to visual information at the expense of purely functional information. This quality is achieved quite effortlessly by splitting up the "figurine" and scattering it over different parts of the driving area. At the outset, this notation was designed for the essentially figural art form of ballet, but is now also used in contemporary dance. It is striking how warmly this notation has been received by the young generation of French choreographers, who excellently reproduce its graphic and gestural aspects in the service of light, peripheral aesthetic principles.

Eskhol-Wachmann, *Movement Notation*, Israel, 1958

This system, one of the most well known in the world of art and science, owes its existence to the encounter of two personalities, the dancer Noa Eskhol and the architect Abraham

Wachmann, both of whom were in search of a vision of movement which would be both all-encompassing and scientific in character.

Eskhol, educated in dance in England, was familiar with the notation of Laban. She adopted several of Laban's principles in her own notation, in particular the device of the centrifugally operating diagram, which, however, she reduced to a horizontal line of vision. The matrix figure of movement here consists in the "cone," which places all driving expression in a perspective which is both spherical and flat, and which enables us to avoid treating the third dimension as a figure which has been merely added as an appendage.

Movement is therefore indicated by means of numerical figures, in an extremely precise, even quantifiable manner, making this system an exception to the rule in the history of notation.

SYSTEMS OF NOTATION WITH COMPUTERS

Computer aids took over from paper "aids" around the year 1960. The use of the word "aid" is deliberate here, because, as far as perception and the system itself are concerned, it remains as yet rather unreasonable to assume that computers contribute a genuinely new way of thinking, and new systems. The innovation introduced by computers can be best appreciated in terms of equipment, providing easy accessibility and the capacity to store information while working. Above all, computers have incited new research into the methods of symbolizing notation.

One could observe early on that each experimental stage in choreographic notation was based on a system of notation which already existed on paper, and this even applied to the fundamental conception of computer software in this field. However, the new variety of methods, the evolving character of scores, and the different electronic codes for writing signs, which ranged from programing, to developing a graphical representation of information, to pure simulation, opened up many interesting and promising perspectives which could be applied to scientific purposes.

However, the future for scores devised on the basis of computers will most likely rely less on systems than on the personal research of people like Marc Matos, who probes into forms of programing software to be used for notation.

The following information, some of which refers to specific systems and, in particular, to the first experiments performed in this field, has been made accessible to us thanks to the work of Ann Hutchinson-Guest.

Michael Noll, *Bell Telephone Laboratories*, New Jersey, 1964

By drawing inspiration from the procedures developed by Marey, Noll came up with the idea of recording the movement of a light source worn by dancers performing in the dark. The film of these events is translated into electronic data, which can then be transcribed into almost any standard system of notation, on the basis of parameters determined by the computer.

According to Hutchinson-Guest, this pro-

ject aimed to go beyond the technological capabilities characteristic of its time, as a result of which Noll was merely confined to translating the data recorded into the form of information graphs, with the help of "stick-figures" (pictograms) represented on a perspectival grid.

John Landsown, *Computer Art Society*, London, 1974

Landsown, an architect and plastician, who was already familiar with computer-assisted creation, applied Benesh notation in order to imagine dance scores which might more closely resemble suggestions indicating how a dancer might move, rather than a complete form of notation. Movements are selected according to "key-frames" similar to those found in techniques used by animators, and consist in suggestions in the form of a series of vignettes, dispensing with intermediary phrases.

It is well known that, in contemporary dance, especially since Marey and Duchamp, the most important feature consists in the "passing" from one position to another. It becomes evident, therefore, that this procedure draws on material which most closely relates to classical ballet.

However, the stroboscopic, jerky aspect of this work does tend to conjure up the aesthetics of French dance in the 1980s, which frequently modeled itself on methods used in animation, and comic strips showing the rapid switch from one key movement to another.

A recent example of this is a piece by Patrick Bossati and Alain Lombard, *Mana danse de nada*, which called on the dancer to invent a movement connecting two positions determined beforehand in the form of a drawing, this also being a technique involving similar procedures to those of animation (1990).

Heinz von Foerster, *Biological Computer Lab*, University of Illinois, 1970

As a follower of Eskhol-Wachmann notation, von Foerster sought to establish a rigorous means of describing movement which would lend itself to being transformed scientifically into mathematical data. This research was essentially destined to serve scientific and military aims, including those of the U.S. Army and the military forces of Israel. At the same time, however, a "dancer" program was also to be brought into operation, in order to transform purely scientific kinetic parameters into choreographic forms of information.

Gordon J. Savage and Jillian M. Officer, *Dep. of Systems Design*, University of Waterloo, Canada, 1977

For the first time ever, practicing dancers took action in the field of computers by applying the findings of Laban and Stepanov in order to perfect software suitable for teaching and interpreting a system of notation. With the use of a digital tablet, the consultant is able to compose a choreographic "menu," which the computer then transforms into notation.

Computer Assisted Instructional Laboratory, University of Pennsylvania, 1978

Having been taken over and quickly developed by the Department of Dance at the University of Iowa, this program made considerable headway with innovations in the representation of the body. The stick-figure, which operates mainly on the basis of levers, was replaced by a "bubble-man," consisting in a film of emulsion which was constantly in motion, circulating over its anthropomorphic shape. Greatly influenced by Laban, this representation was to interest a lot of dancers at the time.

Zella Wolosky, Tom W. Calvert, John Chapman, Afta Pathla, Thecla Shiphorst, *Simon Frazer University*, Vancouver, Canada, 1990

The research projects featured in this work were carried out from 1974 onwards with a "MacLaban" computer system, employing software devised on Apple hardware with the support of dancers and specialists in kinesiology. Its function is to facilitate the continuous memorizing of information relating to the analysis of movement, and can be used as an aid for composition. The product of this system is the machine called "Compose," which was put at the disposal of Merce Cunningham in 1990. Just as the master choreographer previously composed by using traditional aleatory methods (yi-king, among others), "Compose" enables him to choose between all the possible variations of movement and spatial combinations, without it being necessary to have live dancers on hand.

"Compose" functions on the basis of stick-figures or "ring-men," which more closely resemble "bubble-men" than the traditional, articulated pictogram. A demonstration given by Thecla Shiphorst within the framework of the conference "Perception, Movement, Speed," organized by Marseille Objective Dance in December 1990, confirmed the fact that the variations of movement offered by "Compose" are limitless, and possibly exceed

those imaginable for the human mind, the mind which, according to Cunningham, had up till then been the sole limit to the ever expanding scope of choreographic invention.

However, the figurative means of representation, the preservation of a certain perspectivism, superimposed by the codes of a checkerboard floor-plan, the recourse to "keyframes," which were thought to have been long since superseded, all these things have not failed to be a source of disappointment, both on an artistic and conceptual level.

As in other computer-assisted creative fields, it appears that machines have the detrimental effect of introducing a degree of archaism, which is no doubt due less to the machines themselves than to the fascination they bring to bear on their users.

Nevertheless, Cunningham's first computer-assisted choreography, "Trackers," sets an example, a measuring stick with which to probe the question as to whether we actually know how to present machines with genuinely artistic problems. Are we not, perhaps like

dance masters of the fifteenth century, still far from inventing true signs, finding ourselves stuck in the old pursuit of corporeal truth, where signs, regardless of their nature, merely serve as intermediate means to render this truth in a new form?

Department of Dance, University of Ohio, 1991

First commercial presentation of a program offering to teach, and put into direct practice, Laban notation.

The "Labanwriter" does not claim to replace the writer of notation, whose kinesthetic responses to movement are irreplaceable (as long as artificial intelligence, and its complementary artificial corporality, have not been perfected). This system does, however greatly speed up the writing of scores, a prolonged and meticulous job which requires as long as six months from start to finish. This apparatus could put together scores such as those commissioned by recently formed companies, which are often put

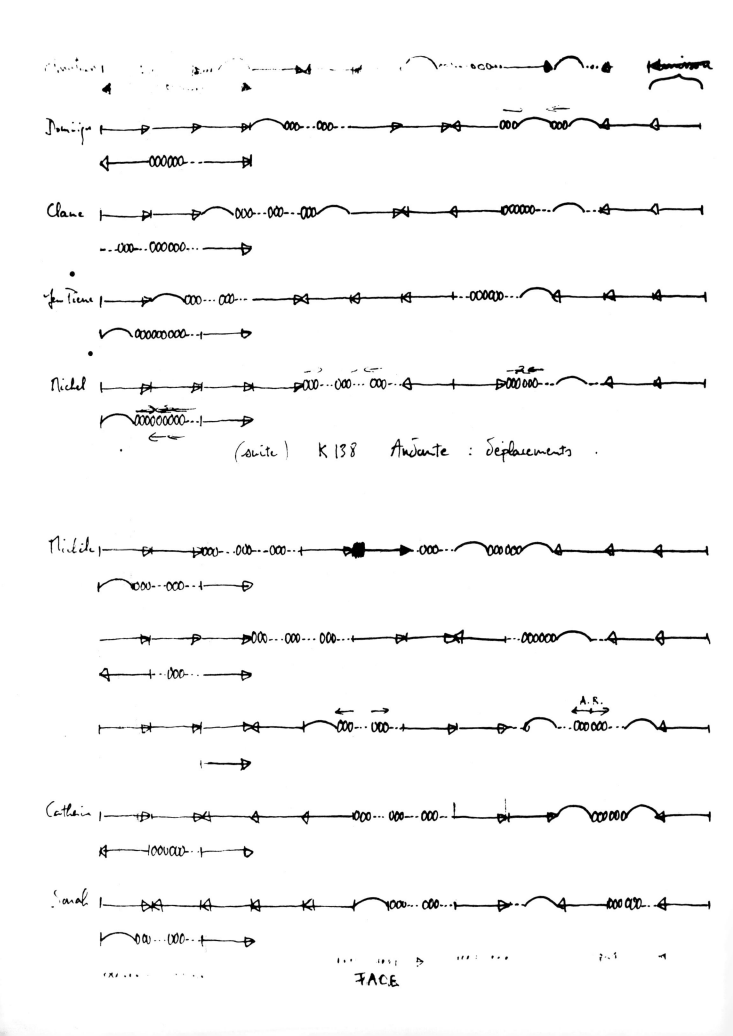

(suite) K 138 Andante : déplacements

FACE

off by the cost of notation. It could also reduce the voluminous corpus of dance archives.

Macbenesh Program, University of Waterloo & Benesh Institute, 1988

The development of a "Benesh" program has been undertaken with the use of Apple Macintosh equipment. This gives direct access to symbolization in Benesh code, and the possibility to accelerate methods of writing and easily store scores. This system was used by Dany Levêque to record Hervé Robbe's choreography, *Appassionnata*, onto floppy disc in 1991.

DRAWINGS

The dawning of the twentieth century brought with it the birth of major systems of notation which later enabled movement to take on a field of autonomous signification which is independent of language. At the same time, however, proceeding along the lines of what appeared to be exactly the opposite trend,

dancers and choreographers adopted individual, and often secret pictorial practices. Like twentieth century painters, modern dancers emancipated themselves from the canons of traditional representation. From this moment on, they presented a singular expression of their being, and of their artistic and spiritual quest, even if this meant deliberately identifying themselves with one of the collective trends which played a formative role in breaking with tradition. Their drawings and notations were later to bear the mark of this new tendency. They proved to be varied in nature, heterogeneous like modern art itself. Sometimes, the art of dance, and the very configuration of its integral parts, could be seen to reflect mysterious analogies with related concomitant practices in the field of plastic arts, music, and architecture.

The interesting characteristic of choreographers' drawings lies in their capacity to serve as a bridge between different states, and different functions, which constantly modify the nature of the viewpoint, or view-

points, of people contemplating them. Such viewpoints give rise to visual dreams, wanderings of the line on a surface, onto which the body may project its own identity, and are never, therefore, entirely detached from the preoccupations of daily life. Whether sketches, grids, notations, landscapes, or paintings, all are permeated with the labor of choreographic invention like an ultimate anxiety which no amount of traces on the page could ever hope to allay.

Eclosion, explosion: Like a gush of energy freeing both space and body, the first modernistic drawings of the twentieth century, by Nijinski, then by the German school (Laban, Wigman), brought about a process of explosion within figures made up of material objects. With the aid of a continuous spherical circular motion, Nijinski turns the universe into a moving spiral, where the center of the figure creates a constant winding and unwinding motion until the zones of the outer contour are set in a permanent state of involution.

◄ 56

The presence of the woman as the driving force behind these ovoid circulations reflects a universe in a state of constant organic metamorphosis, whose choreographic representations are fragmented, jerky, and thus mark what is possibly an insurmountable limit to such representation.

It is curious to note that the similar tempestuous notation of Laban and Wigman led to the "decomposi" subdued turmoils of corporeal dynamics, Laban constructed an "icosahedron," a moving crystal which contained all possible movements within its form. Wigman, on the other hand, extracted from the surface of the page spaces void of any relation to standard scales of reference, where figures tottered on the edge of the invisible abyss of the third dimension, which thus broke them up and drew them down into its depths.

The contribution of the avant-gardes: Under the influence of Fuller, then Duncan, artists at the start of the century endowed dance with the dream of a form of expression free of all sets of codes, and linked to an absolute existential expression of this liberation. From 1910 on, the futurists took an interest in dance as a supreme means in the quest to escape from artistic restraints of the past. The very "Apollonian" Valentine de Saint-Point invented an ultimate poetical work in the form of his "métachorie." Meanwhile, towards 1930, choreographic experiments carried out by Cralli or Prampolino and their interpreters Wy Magoty or Gianina Censi gave form to the famous "aérodanza."

Other "choreographic" initiatives like those of Kandinsky, and several of the Bauhaus artists, were characteristic of the attention paid by painters to this kind of project. Oskar Schlemmer, however, is an exception to this rule, for this painter, sculptor, and man of the theater, applied his experience of dance in order to operate in the true manner of choreographers and give form to a movement with full respect to its inherent structures, on the basis of his authentic experience and knowledge in this field.

Modern and post-modern: The density and proliferation of graphic modes of expression in the American school of contemporary dance from the fifties onwards had the effect of encouraging various tendencies within this rich corpus. Painting approached dance, and vice versa. Whereas painters normally associated with "abstract expressionism" sought to convey via their canvases the sense of urgency of a unique emotion, in the same way as dance aimed to give form to the mysterious content of such urgency, choreographers like Nikolais or Cunningham were to affirm in explicit terms their relation to pictorial representation, and their tendency to adopt some of its categories, and especially the approaches involved in painting. Finally, their quest to establish a more and more refined, accurate definition of the activities specific to dance was soon to be supplanted, in similar fashion to the pictorial avant-gardes, by severe

146

doubt regarding the substantiality of such a clear-cut definition.

The work of Cunningham stands as evidence of this transfer between the "all over" explosion of an off-centered landscape, and the recourse to aleatory practices tending to relativize their inherent lyricism. Opposing the flood of lines flashing across the page, and the animal figures representing the eternal structure of the living, one finds grids in which the carefully contrived possibility of chance persistently perturbs the customary reigning stability.

The following, so-called "post-modern," generation was to extend even further the contrast between the sudden urgency of a corporeal event and the grid of restrictions and trajectories leading to an even, unruffled movement, a steady, neutral vision of the world. It would be quite legitimate to compare Trisha Brown's "quadrigrams" or Lucinda Childs' trajectories, to the cubes created by Donald Judd, the alignments by Carl André, or the mural repetitions by Sol LeWitt. However, one cannot forget that dance is never a statement on reality, but a process. Brown's quadrigram merely guides us, by leveling the movements it suggests, towards the "de-subjectification" of Judd's cube, which embodies elementary forms without narrative, void of any categorial or symbolic supplement. Similarly to the thick "amorphous" sheets of felt by Robert Morris, the drawings of Simone Forti, Yvonne Rainer or Trisha Brown do not formulate anything other than their absence of all external organizing projects.

On the basis of this extreme point of indifference to form, dance practices like those of Meredith Monk or Bob Wilson have given life to an empty universe with an irresolute world of imagination, which will always be left aside from the centralizing, completed projects relating to figures. As painters and moviemakers, as well as choreographers, Monk, and especially Wilson, give form to work which is pictorial in the full sense of the term, and which they consider as such.

Generations of Europe: As a contemporary of the return to narration in the 1980s, the young European school of choreography has clearly been influenced from within by its own heritage of the specific theatrical dance forms originating in Germany. Pina Bausch stands as the major example of this. Choreographic projects can, therefore, take on the form of a story, a scenario, or a story-board. These projects retain, however, in the case of French and Flemish choreographers, the mysterious and secretive character of an intimate biography, the graphic representative of which is often a small figurine in motion, presented on the sheet of paper as a mobile sign of itself. Other scenarios lead us to the heart of densities and expressions of energy (Keersmaeker, Bagouet, Duboc), elements, that is, which no traced line has the capacity to hold in check, unless it admits to representing the trace of *nothing*, a simple work-tool probing the inexpressible, an instrument for measuring and determining the dimensions of the elusive reality of motion.

147

NOTES

PREFACE

1) — A. Hutchinson-Guest: *Dance Notation, the process of recording movement on paper*, Dance Books, London; 1984.

IMPERFECTIONS OF PAPER

1) — Trisha Brown: "Un mystère concret" (translation), in *Bulletin du CNDC* n°5, trans. Denise Luccioni.

2) — Mallarmé, *Crayonné au théâtre*, 1886.

3) — Raymond Bellour, *L'Entre-image*, Editions de la Différence, 1990. (The expression is used in reference to *Nostos II* by Thierry Kuntzell.)

4) — "Then by an exchange whose secret seems to pour from her smile, without delaying she (the dancer) gives over, through the last veil which always remains, the nudity of your concepts, silently writing them in the manner of a Sign, which she is." *Crayonné au théâtre*, op. cit.

5) — Daniel Dobbels, *Martha Graham*, Editions Bernard Coutaz.

6) — The description of these developments goes on until the end of Canto XVIII of Dante *Paradise*, signaling more and more complex figures.

7) — Irgmard Bartenieff, *Body Motion coping with the environment*, Gordon and Beach, N.Y., 1980.

8) — Gilles Deleuze, *Le Pli*, Editions de Minuit, 1990. (The expression designates the monad's "baroque" involution).

9) — Hubert Godard, "A propos des théories sur le mouvement," in *Marsyas*, n°16.

10) — Daniel Dobbels (on the subject of Mary Wigman's drawings): "The stage is a conjured depth that drawing brings back to light... these sketches reveal something no spectator could see, but could only be known in a prescient vision... the empty, unfathomable infernos on which choreography unfurls its unique stage." "Le Sous-sol," in *La Danse, naissance d'un mouvement de pensée*, Armand Colin, 1989.

11) — See the interesting presentation of this exhibition by Ole Henrik Mue: "Ecouter avec les yeux," in *Inharmoniques* n°3.

12) — See "Les mots dans l'art," *Artstudio* n°13.

13) — This is no doubt what Thoinot Arbeau saw already, and with melancholy, at the origin of the difficulty in conserving dance. See "L'injure du Temps et la paresse des hommes" in *Orchésographie*, 1588.

14) — To speak of disinterest is to put it mildly. It is in fact a question of rejection, fear, and sometimes even horror. And this, in all the schools, modern or academic. This rejection calls for numerous studies and debates, which could be nourished by recent events but also by far older ones which have practically the same meaning, in contradictory situations and opposite contexts. Most conservative academic circles, from the Paris Opera to Maurice Béjart, for example, consider the act of notation as an impardonable obstacle to their operations. Not so long ago one of our most distinguished notators saw herself led to the door with threats of physical violence for coming to take down a choreography in writing, at the request of the choreographer himself.

15) — Tamara Karsavine, *Theater Street*, Heinemann, 1930.

16) — Sami Ali, *L'espace imaginaire*, "collection Tel," Gallimard.

17) — Carles Mas Garcia: "La Baixa dansa al regne de Catalunya i Arago el segle XV," in *Nassare Rivista Aragonesca di Musicologia*, IV (1 and 2), 1988. Mas Garcia defines these extraordinary forms as a cross between "the schematic and the imaged."

18) — Choreographic notation, like the activity of composition in space, would seem to be an exclusive characteristic of Western culture. One must point, however, to the existence of certain representations (if not actual notations) of dance in traditions outside our own. One such is the symbolization of the "adavus" of baratha-natyam, transmitted by the large body of iconography proposed in Indian classical statuary, considered as a repertory of postures (see P. Subrahmanyam, "Baratha-nathyam, Indian Classical Dance," in *Marg Publications*, Bombay 1979).

Another may have been discovered

en suitte vous faites chacun deux
pas de menuet en avant, en vous
tenant la main Comme vous le
voyez écrit ci dessous

deux pas de menuet en avant pour l'homme

deux pas de menuet en avant pour la demoiselle

Deuxieme Figure

in the research of Ms. Feng Shuer Liu, "A documental, historical, and analytical study of Chinese Ritual and Ceremonial Dance from the Second Millenium to the Sixth Century b.C.." (thesis presented at the Laban Center, typed copy, archives of the Laban Center, London, 1986).

Certain oracular bones bearing signs that may indicate choreographic elements are considered by this dancer/researcher as prefigurations of choreographic notation.

However, given the importance of gestural and motor elements in the Chinese alphabet, can these grammatical matrixes really be considered distinct from ideogrammatic procedures? Let us merely recall the commentary by Marcel Granet, remarking the difference between the highly corporealized verbal writings of East Asia and the dryness of our purely indexical alphabets: "The Chinese do not separate the art of language from other procedures of signalization and action," in *La Pensée Chinoise*. This study, which is totally fascinating, seems to be in agreement with that of Leroi-

Gourhan: "Figurative, sonorous, and gesticulatory rhythmicity probably emerged in the course of genealogical development, along with language, synchronically with the development of the different techniques." *La parole et le geste*, (vol. 2: "La mémoire et le rythme").

19) — Abaco or the art of mathematics and of measure so important in the Quattrocento is not so far removed from the concomitant invention of choreography as "misura di terreno," in Ebreo's words. See M. Baxandall, *L'oeil du Quattrocento*, Gallimard, 1987.

20) — See W. Kaiser: *La doctrine du langage naturel chez Jacob Boheme*, in Poétique n°11, 1972. And, of course, Michel Foucault, *Les Mots et les Choses*, Gallimard, 1966.

21) — Entretiens avec Bonnie Bainbridge Cohen, translation by Recherche en Mouvement pour la Fédération française de la danse, 1988.

22) — "These characters, letters, and alphabets, the same that God has incorporated here and there in the Bible (a probable allusion to the cryptic codes known as gématrie),

are printed quite readably in His marvelous creations of the heavens and the earth, and even in all the animals... From these letters we have borrowed our magic writing, and we have constituted a new language at the same time; the nature of everything is expressed and explained." *Confession des Rose-Croix*, 1615, quoted in W. Kaiser, op. cit.

Need we recall that Father Mersenne, who elaborated a cosmic theory of the ballet in his *Harmonie Universelle* (1636), also had in view the creation of a "natural" and "universal" writing? On his debate with Descartes over this point, see J. Derrida, *De la Grammatologie*, Editions de Minuit, 1967.

23) — See in this volume the study by Jean-Noel Laurenti, and in a more general way, Michel Foucault, Les Mots et les Choses, op. cit.

24) — *The Art of Dancing, Poem in Three Cantos*, London, 1725.

25) — "The outside, spatial and objective exteriority, which we believe we know as the most familiar thing in the world, as familiarity

itself, would not appear without the gram, without the non-presence of the other that is inscribed in the meaning of the present, without the relationship to death as the concrete structure of the living present." J. Derrida, op. cit.

LIVING SCORES

1) — Etienne Labeyrie, "Groupes Humains et Catastrophes" in R.S/S.I. (Volume 7, n°1), Montreal, March 1987.

NOTATION AND DRAWINGS

1) — Following the initiative of the Dance Notation Bureau, the Hong Kong Center of the Academy for the Performing Arts organized an international conference on dance in June 1990, which approached in depth the problem of notation. Michèle Nadal represented France on behalf of the Conté Système .

FEUILLET'S THINKING

1) — In *Des ballets anciens et modernes selon les règles du théâtre*, 1682.

2) — In England, see Pemberton's

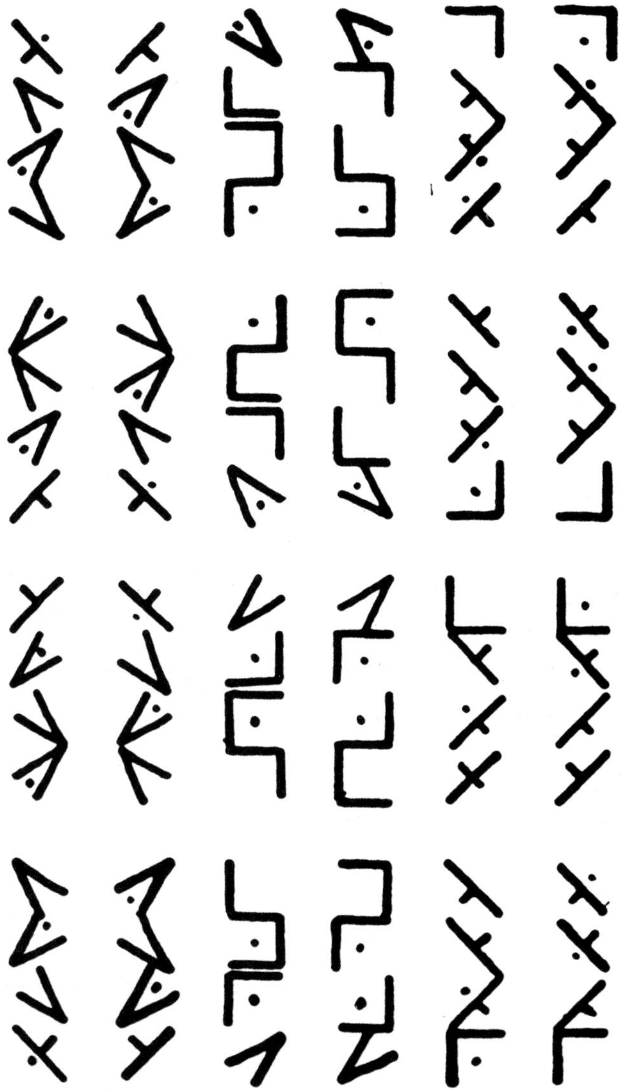

Essay for the Improvement of Dancing (1711), and in Spain, Minguet's *Arte de danzar*, which reproduces, without any indication of authorship, the figures traced by Feuillet's *Ballet de neuf danceurs*, but totally neglects the steps!

3) — On the "academic movement," see Jean-Marie Apostolidès, *Le Roi-machine*, Editions de Minuit, 1981, pp. 23 sqq.

4) — In the petition brought before the royal council in 1704. On the Beauchamps-Feuillet-Lorin affair, see Jean-Michel Guilcher, "André Lorin et l'invention de l'écriture chorégraphique," *Revue de l'histoire du théâtre*, 3ʳᵈ trimester, 1969.

5) — "P" for "pas" [step], "b" for "pas de bourrée," etc.

6) — In the *Abrégé de la nouvelle méthode d'écrire toutes sortes de danses de ville*.

7) — See the "Délibération de l'Académie Royale de Danse," in the *Mercure de France* of August 10, 1731.

8) — Ferriol y Boxerhaus refers to him in his *Reglas utiles para los aficionados a danzar*, Naples, 1745.

9) — Published in Naples in 1728.

10) — See above, note 2.

11) — *Lettres sur la danse*, 1760, VIII, "De la chorégraphie."

12) — *Eléments de chorégraphie*, 1762.

13) — Genarro Magri, *Trattato teorico-prattico di ballo*, Naples, 1779.

14) — Indeed, letter VIII is ambiguous: after having energetically condemned choreography, Noverre accords it a fairly considerable role, on the condition that it be backed up by drawing. This ambiguity is found throughout the *Lettres sur la danse*: faced with the degeneration of ballet, which in his time was conceived as purely ornamental, Noverre presents himself as an innovator; but he seems to link back to the figurative ideal expressed in the seventeenth century. In certain respects, his aesthetic of the passions refers to classical aesthetics; in others, no doubt through the influence of a certain interpretation of English empiricism, he opens the gates to the aesthetics of the characteristic quality which will inform romanticism and realism. This ambiguity is frequent in Encyclopedist circles.

15) — This explains the story told by Noverre, according to which Blondy, disciple of Beauchamps though he was, forbade his students to read the *Chorégraphie*.

16) — A "mouvement", in the terminology of the period, is constituted by the succession of a bend and a rise or a spring.

17) — *Discours de la méthode*, part II.

18) — In fact, the objective is not perfectly attained. For example, the rise [*élévé*] is defined as "lifting" the knees. But how to distinguish the flat (or tense) rise from the stretch on a half-point [*demi-pointe*]? In the second edition of the *Chorégraphie*, in 1701, Feuillet adds tables for a "Supplement of Steps," wherein the problem is addressed, but without any clear solution in our eyes.

19) — One finds this type of correction for the rigadoon step in Rameau's *Maître à danser* (1725), and to an almost systematic extent in the tradition represented by Tomlinson's *The Art of Dancing*.

20) — These examples are taken from the jig of Feuillet's *Polyxène et Pyrrhus*, contained in the dossier *Rés. 817* of the library of the Paris Opera. If one wishes to be perfectly precise, it must be said that the half-measure which prepares the falling step [*pas tombé*] is a *posé sur demi-pointe*, unlike the posé of the galliard, which is done flat footed.

21) — At the crossroads of literature and dance, the 2ⁿᵈ century writer Lucian, widely read in the seventeenth century, and an expert in imitation, explains that the ballet master must possess a vast and varied erudition. His opuscule, *De Saltatione*, is constantly quoted by the theorists.

22) — "The knees bend as though their strength was failing." *Maître à danser*, pp. 143 and 240.

23) — In the same way, by fleshing out the sign for a quarter turn, Rameau's "Nouvelle Méthode" did away with its strictly figurative character.

24) — "The value of the letters is purely negative and differential; thus the same person can write 't' with variants... The only essential thing is that his writing does not confound this sign with the 'l,' the 'd,' etc." "The means of producing the sign is

completely indifferent, for it has no bearing on the system." F. de Saussure, *Cours de linguistique générale*, Payot, pp. 165-66.

25) — *A New Collection of Dances*, composed by L'Abbé (undated).

26) — For this reason it is difficult to take the incomplete choreographies found in the dossier *Rés. 817* of the Paris Opera Library as the traces of a creation stopped short in its tracks. These documents present only the dancers' paths, very neatly marked; this implies that the person who began this work already had the entire choreography at his disposal, with the signs of the steps on the paths, for otherwise the likelihood of distortions in the layout of the paths would make such neatness quite useless. It is probable that this is a working copy (either by Feuillet, or by a secretary) which was never finished.

27) — *Essai sur l'origine des langues*, II.

28) — "It is but sweet and gracious movement, which does not unsettle from the body this pleasing air that is so esteemed and widespread in our Nation." *Maître à danser*, p. 107.

29) — *L'art du ballet de cour en France*, 1581-1643, Editions du C.N.R.S., 1963, pp. 49 sqq.

30) — The second volume, published in 1610, blends druidism with the discovery of secret temples of gallantry.

31) — See Didier Kahn, "L'Alchimie sur la scène française au XVIᵉ et XVIIᵉ siècles," in *Chrysopœia*, J.C. Bailly, Paris, January/March 1988, pp. 67 sqq.

32) — See Boileau, *Art Poétique*, III, verses 160-244.

33) — For seventeenth-century minds, the two are not necessarily contradictory: witness a man like Boileau, an admirer of Pascal and a friend of the Jansenists while also a defender of the pagan marvelous. But the attitude which L. Goldmann, in *Le Dieu caché*, calls the "worldly refusal of the world" will become untenable at the moment when the order of the mind claims all the rights from the order of charity, and reason no longer cedes anything to the heart.

34) — The expression is used by Charles Pauli in *Les Eléments de la danse*, Leipzig, 1756.

35) — As demonstrated by the two versions of Feuillet's *Folies d'Espagne* and by L'Abbé's two versions of the passacaglia in *L'Armide*, certain choreographies could be adapted either for one soloist or for a couple. But to imagine the movement of an entire ballet troupe on this basis is quite another thing.

36) — This seems to be the origin of the solist's supremacy and specialization in a given type of dance, against which Noverre so loudly protests. But the exact dates of this phenomenon remain uncertain.

37) — "The art of describing dance only extends to simple dance, and not to the art of gesture." Pauli, op. cit., note 34, p. 75.

38) — Preface to the *Art de toucher le clavecin*.

LABAN, SCHOENBERG, KANDINSKY

1) — Wigman changed the spelling of her name in 1919 when she commenced her independent career as a performing artist.

2) — Physical culture was a widespread movement for the promotion of a sense of well-being through practical exercise, supported by government funding, with several competing and complementary systems.

3) — Suzanne Perrottet was a young Swiss Dalcroze teacher who, dissatisfied with the strictness of his system, was attracted to Laban's work, joining him in 1913. She remained a Laban teacher all her life in Zurich.

BIBLIOGRAPHY

BARBICAN ART GALLERY, *A Golden Age: Art and Society in Hungary 1896-1914*; catalogue of the exhibition of the same title at the Barbican Art Galery, October 1989 - January 1990
BARTENIEFF IRMGARD, *Body Movement coping with the Environnement*, Gordon & Breach, New-York, 1980 *Feuillet, l'Art d'écrire la Danse*, in Dance Notation Record, vol.7, 1956.
BENESH RUDOLF, *Reading Dance, the Birth of Choreology*, Souvenir Press, London, 1977
BOLLIGER HANS, MAGNAGVAGNO GUIDO, MEYER RAIMOND, *Dada in Zürich*, Kunsthaus Zürich und Arche Verlag, Zürich, 1985
BRANDENBURG HANS, *Der Moderne Tanz*, Georg Müller, München, 1st éd. 1913; 2nd éd. 1917 « Erinnerungen an Labans Anfänge », *Schrifttanz* 2. Jg, Heft IV, Dec 1929
CHALLET-HAAS JACQUELINE, *Manuel Elémentaire de Cinétographie Laban*, several volumes, 1963/81/87
CONTE PIERRE, *Technique Générale d'Ecriture*, Arts et Mouvement, Paris, 1957
Danses Anciennes de Cour et de Théâtre en France, Dessain et Tolra, Paris, 1974
DUQUESNE MONIQUE, *La Chaconne de Phaéton (Feuillet-Conté)*, Mémoire de 3ème cycle, Univ. de Paris IV, 1989
FRY EDWARD F., *Cubism*, Thames and Hudson, London, 1966
FUCHS GEORG, *Die Revolution des Theaters: Ergebnisse aus dem Münchener Künstlertheater*, Georg Müller, Munich and Leipzig, 1909
GREEN MARTIN, *Moutain of Truth/The Counter Culture Begins, Ascona 1900-1920*, Univ. Press of New England, Hanover et London, 1986
GROPIUS WALTER, *The Theatre of the Bauhaus*, Wesleyan Univ. Press, Middletown, Conn., 1961
GUILCHER JEAN-MICHEL, «André Lorin et l'invention de l'écriture chorégraphique», in *Histoire du Théâtre*, Paris, Oct-Déc. 1969
HILTON WENDY, *Dance of Court and Theater*, Princeton Books, Princeton, 1981, (Feuillet-Laban)
HAHL-KOCH JELENA, *Arnold Schönberg, Wassily Kandinsky — Letters, Pictures and Documents*, Faber and Faber, London, 1984
HODIN J.P., *Oskar Kokoschka:The Artist and His Time*, Cory, Adams and Mackay, London, 1966
HOFSTÄTTER HANS H., *Art Nouveau/Prints, Illustrations and Posters*, Omega Books, London, 1984
HUELSENBECK RICHARD, *Dada Almanach*, Something Else Press, New-York, 1966
HUTCHINSON-GUEST ANN, *Dance Notation, the Process of Recording Dance on Paper*, Dance Books, London, 1984

JELAVICH PETER, *Munich and Theatrical Modernism: Politics, Playwriting and Performance*, Harvard Univ. Press, Cambridge, Mass., 1985
KANDINSKY WASSILY, MARC FRANZ, *Der Blaue Reiter*, R. Piper & Co, Munich, 1912
KANDINSKY WASSILY, *Concerning the Spiritual in Art*, Dover, New-York, 1977 (orig. 1914)
KLEE FELIX, *The Diaries of Paul Klee 1898-1918*, Univ.of California Press, Berkeley, Calif, 1964
KNUST ALBRECHT, *Handbook of Kinetography Laban - Dictionary of Kinetography Laban*, Mac-Donald & Evans, London, 1979
LABAN RUDOLF VON, *Die Welt des Tänzers*, Chr. Belserschen Buchdruckerei, Stuttgart, 1920
Choreographie, Eugen Diederichs Verlag, Jena, 1926
Des Kindes Gymnastik und Tanz, Gerhardt Stalling Verlag, Oldenburg, 1926
Schrifttanz : Methodik, Orthographie, Erläuterungen, Universal-Edition, Vienna, 1928
Gymnastik und Tanz, Gerhardt Stalling Verlag, Oldenburg, 1929
Ein Leben für den Tanz, Carl Reissner Verlag, Dresden, 1935
Laban's Principles of Dance and Movement Notation, Macdonald & Evans, London, 1975.
The Mastery of Movement, Macdonald & Evans, re-ed. 1988.
LANCELOT FRANCINE, «L'écriture de la danse, le système Feuillet», in *Revue d'Ethnologie Française* n°1, 1972.
LENMAN ROBIN, *Censorship and Society in Munich, 1890-1914*, D. Phil diss. University of Oxford, 1975
« Politics and Culture: The State and the Avant-Garde in Munich, 1886-1914 », in R.J Evans, *Society and Politics in Wilhelmine Germany*, Croom Helm, London, 1978
LINDSAY KENNETH C., VERGO PETER, *Kandinsky - Complete Writings on Art*, (tome 1: 1901-1921) and (vol 2: 1922-1943), Faber and Faber, London, 1982
MARSYAS, *Revue de l'IPMC* n°6, « notations musicales et chorégraphiques ».
MAS GARCIA CARLES, «La Baixa Dansa al regne de Catalunya y Arago el segle XV», in *Rev. Nassare*, Sarragosse, 1988
PATTERSON MICHAEL, *The Revolution in German Theatre*, Routledge & Kegan Paul, London, 1981
PAVIS PATRICK, «Réflexion sur la notation et la mise en scène théâtrale», in *Revue. d'histoire du Théâtre*, Oct-Dec.1981
POMARES JEAN, «Le Plaisir du texte», in *Théâtre Public* n°58-59, Summer 1984

PRESTON-DUNLOP VALERIE, *Readers in Kinetography Laban* (2 volumes: series A et B), Macdonald & Evans, London, 1967
RICHARD LIONEL, *The Concise Encyclopedia of Expressionism*, Omega Books, Ware, Herts, reimp. 1986
RITCHER HANS, *Dada, Art and Anti-Art*, Oxford University Press, New-York, 1965
ROAZEN PAUL, *Freud and His Followers*, New American Library, New-York, 1976
SCHLEMMER OSKAR, *The Letters and Diaries of Oskar Schlemmer*, translat. Winston Krisham, Wesleyan Univ. Press, Middleton, Conn., 1972
SCHÖNBERG ARNOLD, *Harmonielehre*, Universal-Edition, Vienna, 1911
Pierrot Lunaire Op. 21, Universal-Edition, Vienna, 1914
SEGEL HAROLD B., *Turn-of-the-Century Cabaret*, Columbia Univ. Press, New-York, 1987
SMITH JOAN ALLEN, *Schönberg and His Circle: A Viennese Portrait*, Schirmer Books, New-York et Collier Macmillan, London, 1986
SORELL WALTER, *The Mary Wigman Book: Her Writings*, Wesleyan Univ. Press, Middletown, Conn. 1975
STEIN ERWIN, *Arnold Schönberg Letters*, Faber and Faber, London, 1964
STUCKENSCHMIDT H.H, *Schönberg : His Life. World and Work* (trad. Humphrey Searle), Schirmer Books, New-York, 1978
SZEEMANN HARALD, *Monte Verità*, Electra Editrice, Milan, 1978
VOLBOUDT PIERRE, *Kandinsky*, Art Data, Angleterre, 1986
WARNER MARY JANE, *International Bibliography: Labanotation Scores*, (diffusé par le CNEM), 1984-1988.
WASHTON LONG ROSE-CAROL, *Kandinsky: The Development of an Abstract Style*, Clarendon Press, Oxford, 1980
WEISS PEG, *Kandinsky in Munich: The Formative Jugendstil Years*, Princeton Univ. Press, Guilford, 1979
WELLESZ EGON, *Arnold Schönberg*, Greenwood Press, Westport, Conn., re-printed. 1970 (orig. 1925)
WILLET JOHN, *The New Sobriety 1917-1933/Art and Politics in the Weimar Period*, Thames & Hudson, London, 1978
WINTHER F.H., *Körperbildung als Kunst und Pflicht*, Delphin-Verlag, Munich, 3rd ed. augmented 1919

silence   charnière

D.   C.   Mle   A   Sau   JP.   M.   N.   Cl.

petit pied
tmp lu
cellulite
mache

NOTATION ORGANIZATIONS

Laban Notation
NAME OF SYSTEM: LABONOTATION (ENGLAND) - CINETOGRAPHIE (FRANCE)

Kinetographisches Institut
Folkwang Hochschule, Fachbereich 3
Essen
This prestigious school of modern dance was founded by Kurt Jooss and Sigurd Leeder at the same time as Laban himself was actively working on notation. It lays claim not only to having schooled Pina Bausch in dance, but also to being one of the first institutes to offer courses in notation.

Laban Centre for Movement and Dance
Goldsmith College, University of London
Laurie Crove, New Cross
London SE14 6NW
This renowned school is an independent organization which offers artistic and theoretical teaching in dance, as well as in notation. Archives, and a well-equipped library are at the disposal of students and researchers alike. This center is also authorized to award doctoral degrees, and to supervise research.

The Language of Dance Centre
17 Holland Park
London W11 3DT
A center offering access to important archives and documentation.

Centre for Dance Studies
Les Bois/St Peter
Jersey - Channel Islands
Roederick Lange, the coordinator of this insular cell of kinetography, publishes an excellent journal, Dance Studies, which is devoted particularly to the study of traditional dance and to theoretical problems of notation.

The Dance Notation Bureau
33 W 21 Street
New York, N.Y. 10011
A prestigious sanctuary of notation, where some of Laban's students took refuge in exile from Nazi Germany, and began to write down the major work of Modern Dance in the thirties.

Department of Dance (College of the Arts)
Ohio State University
1813 High Street
Columbus, Ohio 43210
Among the famous dance departments of American universities, that of Ohio Suni is one of the most important as far as theoretical activities are concerned, in particular thanks to the presence of Vera Maletic. Columbus is also the home of the International Council of Kinetography Laban, coordinated by Lucy Venable, head of the "Labanwriter" program.

Akademia Népzenei
Intézete Néptànc Osztàly
1014 Budapest
As in most eastern European countries, the Hungarian exponents of notation have devoted themselves particularly to recording popular dance.

Centre National d'Ecriture du Mouvement
Place Saint-Arnould
60800 Crépy en Valois
Jacqueline Challet-Haas, assisted by Marion Bastien, represents the heart and soul of French kinetography. The CNEM awards a professional diploma, and its teaching now forms part of several higher education degree courses in France. A large proportion of its activities consist in writing records of the latest French contributions to choreography.

Benesh System
NAME OF SYSTEM: CHOREOLOGY

The Benesh Institute of Choreology
4, Margravine Gardens
London W6 8RH
&
Jean Romarès
Théâtre Contemporain de la Danse
9, rue Geoffroy l'Asnier
75004 Paris
This temple of Benesh notation awards a professional diploma, complemented by practical courses with dance companies. A twin version of this system has been set up in France. Activities concentrate on teaching, but also on notating current choreographic creations.

Conté System
NAME OF SYSTEM: ECRITURE DU MOUVEMENT

Association Ecriture du Mouvement
7, rue du Dragon
75006 Paris
On the basis of Michèle Nadal's teaching, several writers of Conté notation have established themselves in France. They mostly teach in the academies ("conservatoires"), and within the scope of some university degree courses in dance, like the one in Nice. The association also publishes Conté's writings.

Eskhol-Wachmann System
NAME OF SYSTEM: MOVEMENT NOTATION

The Movement Notation Society
75 Arlozorov Street
Holon, Israel
This society stands on the fringe of Eskhol Dance Company, and pursues a strange and sublime line of reflection on the movement of living things, human or animal.

60 ▶

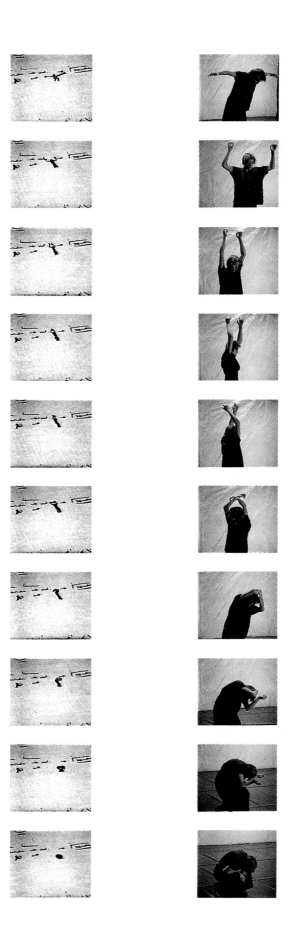

PHOTOS INDEX